REINCARNATION

A STUDY IN HUMAN EVOLUTION

THE RESURRECTION OF THE BODY

AND THE REINCARNATION OF THE SOUL

DR. TH. PASCAL

TRANSLATED BY FRED ROTHWELL

1st WORLD
LIBRARY
Literary Society

Reincarnation

Th. Pascal

© 1st World Library, 2007
PO Box 2211
Fairfield, IA 52556
www.1stworldlibrary.com
First Edition

LCCN: 2007930822

Softcover ISBN: 978-1-4218-4861-7
Hardcover ISBN: 978-1-4218-4764-1
eBook ISBN: 978-1-4218-4958-4

Purchase *"Reincarnation"*
as a traditional bound book at:
www.1stWorldLibrary.com/purchase.asp?ISBN= 978-1-4218-4861-7

1st World Library is a literary, educational organization
dedicated to:

- Creating a free internet library of downloadable ebooks

- Hosting writing competitions and offering book publishing
scholarships.

Interested in more 1st World Library books? contact:
literacy@1stworldlibrary.com
Check us out at: www.1stworldlibrary.com

1st World Library Literary Society

Giving Back to the World

"If you want to work on the core problem, it's early school literacy."

- James Barksdale, former CEO of Netscape

"No skill is more crucial to the future of a child, or to a democratic and prosperous society, than literacy."

- Los Angeles Times

"Literacy... means far more than learning how to read and write... The aim is to transmit... knowledge and promote social participation."

- UNESCO

"Literacy is not a luxury, it is a right and a responsibility. If our world is to meet the challenges of the twenty-first century we must harness the energy and creativity of all our citizens."

- President Bill Clinton

"Parents should be encouraged to read to their children, and teachers should be equipped with all available techniques for teaching literacy, so the varying needs and capacities of individual kids can be taken into account."

- Hugh Mackay

"Were an Asiatic to ask me for a definition of Europe, I should be forced to answer him:—It is that part of the world which is haunted by the incredible delusion that man was created out of nothing, and that his present birth is his first entrance into life."

—SCHOPENHAUER.

Parerga and Paralipomena, Vol. 2, Chap. 15

CONTENTS

SKETCH OF THE AUTHOR'S LIFE

Theophile Pascal was born on the 11th of May, 1860, at Villecroze, a village in the South of France. His childhood was spent amid the pleasant surroundings of a country life. Shortly after his sixteenth birthday, a relative of his, a Catholic priest ministering in Toulon, seeing that the youth showed considerable ability, sent for him and presided over his studies in this large maritime centre. Before many years elapsed, he entered the Naval Medical School of the town, which he left at the age of twenty-two, with first-class honours. In his professional capacity, he took several trips on vessels belonging to the Mediterranean squadron. Four years afterwards he married, resigned active naval service, and devoted himself to building up a practice on land, becoming a homoeopathic physician in the great seaport itself. It was about this time that the young doctor became interested in Theosophy, owing to the kindly services of a former patient, Commander Courmes. The closest friendship and sympathetic interest in theosophic thought thus began, and continued during their common labours subsequently in Paris, Dr. Pascal entered the Theosophical Society in 1891, and during the course of the following year wrote a series of articles for the *Revue Theosophique Francaise*. These were continued year after year, and dealt with the most varied subjects: Psychic Powers; The Fall of the Angels; Kama-Manasic Elementals; Thought Forms; Christianity, Prehistoric Races, and many others.

The young doctor had previously made a deep study of human magnetism, which proved a most fertile ground for the sowing of the seed of the Ancient Wisdom.

In 1898 attacks of serious nervous depression became frequent, forcing him to cease work of every kind. Mrs. Besant persuaded him to accompany her to India, where his general health was gradually restored, and he was enabled to return to France in the following year.

He decided to leave Toulon, where he had built up a considerable practice, and to settle in Paris, hoping to provide for the needs of himself and his family—his wife and only daughter—by the exercise of his profession, and at the same time to fight the good fight for Theosophy in the capital itself.

The French Section of the Theosophical Society was founded in 1900, and Dr. Pascal was elected General Secretary. Throughout the next two years a number of thoughtful articles and publications appeared from his pen. The incessant labour and attention, however, which he bestowed on the spreading of theosophic instruction began to have its effect on a naturally delicate constitution, and in July, 1902, when attending the meetings of the British Convention in London, he was prostrated by an attack of congestion of the brain. The most devoted care was lavished on him, both in London and in Paris, the result being that a rapid, though only temporary, recovery took place. Had he relaxed his efforts somewhat, the cure might have been a permanent one, but Dr. Pascal, with the penetrating vision of the mystic, saw how pressing were the needs of the age, and how few the pioneers of this new presentation of the Truth, so that, at whatever cost of personal sacrifice, he plunged once more into the midst of his arduous toil.

Th. Pascal

In 1903 a series of very fine articles on the Laws of Destiny appeared in the *Revue Theosophique*, to be followed immediately by publication in volume form. Two years afterwards appeared the present volume—REINCARNATION: A STUDY IN HUMAN EVOLUTION; a work considered the most complete of any that have so far appeared in France on this subject, and the most popular of Dr. Pascal's publications.

In 1906 some of the nerve centres controlling the organs of speech became affected, but not sufficiently to compel him to remain absent from the International Theosophical Congress held that year in Paris under the presidency of Colonel Olcott. It was on this occasion that Dr. Pascal received from the hands of the President-Founder the Subba Rao medal, awarded to members of the society whose literary labours in the promulgation of the truths of Theosophy have proved eminently useful.

Twelve months afterwards he attended the Congress at Munich, under the presidency of Mrs. Besant, but was obliged to leave before the termination of the meetings. This may be regarded as Dr. Pascal's last public appearance as an active theosophist, for his subsequent prolonged stay in the South of France effected no radical improvement in the state of his health.

Returning to Paris in March, 1908, and realising how impossible it was for him to fulfil the duties incumbent on a General Secretary, he decided to resign his post. His colleagues, however, insisted on his continuing as Honorary General Secretary. From this time onward his health became gradually worse, and his physical life terminated on the 18th of April, 1909, his body being cremated three days afterwards at the Cemetery of Pere Lachaise.

What was most striking about Dr. Pascal, in both public and private life, was his intense earnestness—the index of a well-grounded habit of concentration—and the calm strength of his convictions. It was impossible to be in his presence for any length of time without feeling the power that emanated from him, and recognising that here was a mighty soul struggling for expression.

Other characteristics were his extreme modesty, and his continual endeavour to accord praise and merit to those working for the cause so dear to his own heart. When questioned on many of the intricate points raised in a lecture or in conversation on some abstruse theosophical subject, he made no pretence at knowledge he did not possess; on such occasions his confession of ignorance would be charming, even touching in its *naivete*.

But the qualities he seemed to feel it his special object to awaken in the minds of others—as will be acknowledged, I think, by those who knew him best—may be inferred from his continual insistence on the double duty, incumbent on students of Theosophy, of practising on all occasions the utmost tolerance, refusing not only to condemn but even to judge harshly the opinions or actions of others, and of seizing every opportunity to help another because of the recognition of the One Life throughout the world, May we who read the following pages catch somewhat of the deep earnestness and enthusiastic spirit breathing through them, and may the joy of service dissipate all meaner, motives, taking as our watchword also the only key to true growth, the very heart of altruism, that exhortation he never wearied of repeating: *Aidez! Aidez toujours!*

F. R.

AUTHOR'S PREFACE

It will soon be: 1500 years since the decision of the Council of 543 A.D.[1] condemned to oblivion sublime teachings which ought to have been carefully preserved and handed down to future generations as a beacon amid social reefs; teachings that would have uprooted that frightful egoism which threatens to annihilate the world, and instilled patience into the hearts of such as were being crushed beneath the wheel of the cosmic law, by showing them the scales of Justice inclining to the side filled with their iniquities of bygone times; teachings which would have been welcomed by the masses, and the understanding of which would not have called for any lofty intellectual culture.

It was one of the greatest misfortunes that could have befallen the races of the West, more especially the European, that they were thus deprived for centuries of this indispensable knowledge. We look upon it as a duty, following on so many others, to offer it anew, this time in the clear, logical, illuminating form presented in theosophic teachings. The necessity thereof is all the more imperative when we consider the growth of scepticism and materialism amongst the more intellectual classes, whilst the mass of the people have forsaken their blind faith only to succumb to religious indifference.

To every awakened soul the question comes:

Why does evil exist?

So long as the enigma remains unsolved, Suffering remains a threatening sphinx, opposing God and ready to devour mankind.

The key to the secret lies in Evolution, which can be accomplished only by means of the continual return of souls to earth.

When once man learns that suffering is the necessary result of divine manifestation; that inequalities of conditions are due to the different stages which beings have reached and the changeable action of their will; that the painful phase lasts only a moment in Eternity, and that we have it in our power to hasten its disappearance; that though slaves of the past, we are masters of the future; that, finally, the same glorious goal awaits all beings—then, despair will be at an end; hatred, envy, and rebellion will have fled away, and peace will reign over a humanity made wise by knowledge.

Were this modest work to hasten forward this time by a few years, we should feel sufficiently rewarded.

The subject will be divided into four chapters:

(1) The Soul and the bodies.

(2) Reincarnation and the moral law.

(3) Reincarnation and science.

(4) Reincarnation and the religious and philosophical concensus of the ages.

Th. Pascal

FOOTNOTES:

[Footnote 1: This Council came to the following decision:—
Whosoever shall teach the pre-existence of the soul and the strange opinion of its returns to earth, let him be anathema!]

CHAPTER I

THE SOUL AND THE BODIES

In a book dealing with the resurrection of bodies and the reincarnations of the Soul, a chapter must be devoted to the fundamental elements of the question.

We will give the name of *Soul* to abstract Being, to the Unknown, that unmanifested Principle which cannot be defined, for it is above all definition.

It is the Absolute of Western philosophers, the *Parabrahm* of the Hindus, the *Tao* of the ancient sages of China, the causeless Cause of all that has been or ever will be manifested in concrete time and space.

Some feeble idea of it may perhaps be obtained by comparing it with electricity, which, though the cause of various phenomena: heat, movement, chemical action, light, is not, *per se*, any one of these phenomena, undergoes no modification from their existence, and survives them when the apparatus through which they manifest disappears.

We shall set up no distinction between this Soul, which may be called the universal Soul, and the individual soul, which has often been defined as a ray, a particle of the total Soul, for logically one cannot imply parts to the Absolute; it is illusion, limitation on our part, which shows us souls in the Soul.

Bodies are "aspects" of the Soul, results of its activity—if, indeed, the Infinite can be said to be either active or passive; words fail when we attempt to express the Inexpressible. These bodies, or, more precisely, the varied forms assumed by force-matter[2] are aspects of the Soul, just as light or chemical action are aspects of electricity, for one cannot suppose anything outside of infinite Being, nor can anything be imagined which is not a manifestation of the abstract Whole.

Let us also define *Consciousness*.

Taken absolutely, it is Being, the Soul, God; the uncaused Cause of all the states which, in beings, we call states of consciousness.

This limited consciousness may be defined as the faculty a "centre of life" possesses of receiving vibrations from its surroundings. When, in the course of evolution, a being is sufficiently developed to become conscious of a separation between its "I" and the object which sends it vibrations, consciousness becomes self-consciousness. This *self-*consciousness constitutes the *human* stage; it appears in the higher animals, but as it descends the scale of being, gradually disappears in non-individualised consciousness.

In a word, absolute Consciousness is one, though, as in the above example, it is manifested differently, according to the differences in the vehicles which express it in the concrete world in which we live.

The Soul, *per se*, is beyond the reach of beings who have not finished the pilgrimage of evolution. To know it, one must have attained to the eternal Centre, the unmanifested Logos. Up to that point, one can only, in proportion as one ascends, feel it in oneself, or acknowledge it by means of the logic which perceives it through all its manifestations as the universal Mover of forms, the Cause of all things, the Unity that produces diversity by means of the various vehicles which serve it as methods of expression.

Science says that intelligence, or, to be more generic, consciousness, results from the action of matter. This is a mistake.

Consciousness does not change in proportion as the cells of the body are renewed; rather it increases with physical unconsciousness, as in somnambulism.

Thought is not the fruit of the brain; it offers itself to the latter, ready made, so to speak; the loftiest intellectual or artistic inspirations are flashes which strike down into the awaiting brain, when maintaining that passive expectant attitude which is the condition in which a higher message may be received.

The senses are not the thinking-principle. They need to be controlled by consciousness; thus, people blind from birth, when suddenly made to see, cannot judge either distance or perspective; like animals and primitive men, they see nothing but colours on a surface.

Science says also: the organ is created for the function it has to perform; again a mistake. The eyes of the foetus are constructed in the darkness of the womb. The human germ, notwithstanding its unconsciousness and its simplicity of structure, develops a body that is complex and capable of a considerable degree of consciousness; though itself unintelligent, it produces prodigies of intelligence in this body; here, consequently, the effect would be greatly superior to the cause, which is absurd. Outside of the body and the germ is a supreme Intelligence which creates the models of forms and carries out their construction. This Intelligence is the Soul of the world.

If Consciousness *per se*, or the Soul, is above all direct proof at the present stage of human evolution, the vehicles through which it functions are more or less apparent to us provided they are capable of affecting the brain. At the present stage of human evolution, this is the case only with the astral body; the other bodies are too fine to manifest through the nervous system such characteristics as are calculated to furnish scientists with a proof of their existence; they can only be felt and proved in and by *Yoga*.[3]

It is not without importance, however, to set forth the proofs of the existence of a vehicle of consciousness immediately above the physical, for it affords us a wider horizon and throws far more light on the rest of the subject.

PROOFS OF THE ASTRAL BODY

Certain normal and abnormal or morbid phenomena in man have proved the existence of this vehicle, which we will call the *higher* consciousness, for it is far greater than normal, waking consciousness, that of the brain. In the somewhat rare cases in which this consciousness is expressed in the physical world, it is forced to make use of the brain. Now, in the majority of men, the latter is still incapable of vibrating harmoniously with the matter which forms the astral vehicle; this is because the density of the atoms of the brain cells which preside over thought is incapable of reproducing the rapid vibrations of the finer matter belonging to the body immediately above it. By special training (the *yoga* of the Hindus), by a particular constitution of body (*sensitiveness*), by certain special methods (*hypnotism*), or in certain maladies (*somnambulism*), the brain may become receptive to these vibrations, and receive from them an impression, though always an imperfect one. The rarity of this impression, its imperfection, and especially the necessity for the vibration of the physical brain that it may be manifested in our environment; all these have made it very difficult to prove the existence of this higher vehicle; still, there are certain considerations which show that it exists, and that it alone is capable of explaining the most characteristic phenomena of the higher consciousness.

Let us first define these two states of consciousness rather more completely, and fix their limits.

Normal consciousness is that which functions during waking hours, when the brain is in full physiological activity, freely and completely related to the outer physical world. This consciousness is more or less developed according to the individual, but its component parts—sensation, emotion, sentiment, reason, intelligence, will, intuition—do not exceed known limits; for instance, we do not find clairvoyance, the prophetic faculty, and certain other abnormal faculties, which we shall class under the higher consciousness.

The higher consciousness works in the astral body, whether externalised or not; it seldom manifests itself, and then incompletely; it is accompanied by the more or less complete inhibition of the senses, and by a kind of sleep in which the relations of the subject with the physical world are wholly or partially suspended. The characteristics of this state are greater keenness of the normal faculties, and the appearance of new ones, which are often inexplicable and extraordinary and the more remarkable in proportion as sleep is more profound, the brain calmer, or the physiological state more abnormal.

How can we explain the paradox that faculties shown by a brain in a state of inactivity cover an extent of ground which the brain in a state of activity cannot approach? The reason is that the brain, in this case, is not an instrument moved directly by the cause of consciousness, *the soul*, but a simple recipient, which the soul, then centred in the astral body, impresses *on returning to the physical body* (if it has been far away) or impresses directly when, whilst acting in the finer vehicle, the latter has not left the body.[4]

In other words, the brain, by reason of its functional inactivity, vibrates little or not at all in its higher centres; it plays the part of a sounding-board at rest, capable of vibrating sympathetically under the influence of a similar board placed by its side.

The necessity of cerebral quiet, if the higher consciousness is to make an impression, is now easy to understand; the finer vibration of the astral body cannot be impressed upon the brain when the latter is already strongly vibrating under the action of normal consciousness. For this reason also, the deeper the sleep of the physical body the better the higher consciousness manifests itself.

In ordinary man, organic quiet is scarcely ever complete during sleep; the brain, as we shall see shortly, automatically repeats the vibrations which normal consciousness has called forth during the waking state; this, together with an habitual density of the nervous elements, too great to respond to the higher vibration, explains the rarity and the confused state of the impression of astral consciousness on the brain.

The facts relating to the higher consciousness are as

numerous as they are varied. We shall not enter into full details, but choose only a few phenomena quoted in well-known works.

MANIFESTATIONS OF THE HIGHER CONSCIOUSNESS DURING THE DIFFERENT KINDS OF SLEEP

Normal dream. During normal sleep there exists a special consciousness which must not be confounded either with waking consciousness or with that of the astral body. It is due to the automatic, cerebral vibration which continues during sleep, and which the soul examines on its return to the body—when awake. This dream is generally an absurd one, and the reason the dreamer notices it only on awaking is that he is absent from the visible body during sleep.

The proof of the departure of the astral body during sleep has been ascertained by a certain number of seers, but the absurdity of the commonplace dream is a rational proof thereof, one which must here be mentioned. As another rational proof of the existence of a second vehicle of consciousness, we must also notice the regular registering of the commonplace dream, because it takes place in the brain, and the habitual non-registering of the true dream experience, because this latter takes place in the externalised astral body.

Why does the astral body leave the physical during sleep? This question is beyond our power to answer, though a few considerations on this point may be advanced.

Sleep is characterised by the transfer of consciousness from the physical to the astral body; this transfer seems to take place normally under the influence of bodily fatigue. After the day's activity, the senses no longer afford keen sensations, and as it is the energy of these sensations that keeps the consciousness "centred" in the brain[5]; this consciousness, when the senses are lulled to sleep, centres in the finer body, which then leaves the physical body with a slight shock.

It is, however, of the real dream—which is at times so intelligent that it has been called lucid, and at all events is reasonable, logical, and co-ordinate—that we wish to speak. In most cases this dream consists of a series of thoughts due to the soul in action in the astral body; it is sometimes the result of seeing mental pictures of the future[6] or else it represents quite another form of animistic activity, as circumstances and the degree of the dreamer's development permit.

It is in the lucid dream—whether belonging to normal or to abnormal sleep—that occur those numerous and well-known cases of visions past or future to be found in so many of the books dealing with this special subject.

To these same states of higher consciousness are due such productions as Walter Scott's *Ivanhoe*. The author, suffering from fever, wrote this work whilst in a kind of delirious condition; *Ivanhoe* was printed before the recovery of the author, who, on reading it at a later date, had not the slightest recollection that it was his own production. (Ribot's *Maladies de la Memoire*, p. 41.)

Walter Scott remembered nothing, because *Ivanhoe* was the fruit of the astral consciousness impressed upon a brain which fever had rendered temporarily receptive to the higher vibrations.

There are certain peculiarities of the real dream which prove almost mathematically the superior nature of the vehicle which gives expression to it. This dream, for instance, is never of a fatiguing nature, however long it may appear to last, because it is only an instantaneous impression made upon the brain by the astral body, when the latter returns to the physical body, on awaking. On the other hand, the cerebral ideation of the waking state is fatiguing if intense or prolonged, or if the nervous system of the thinker is deprived of its normal power of resistance (*in neurasthenia*); the commonplace (*brain*) dream is also fatiguing if prolonged or at all vivid.

Another peculiarity is that a dream—the real dream—which would require several years of life on earth for its realisation, can take place in a second. The dream of Maury (*Le Sommeil et le Reve*, p. 161), who in half a second lived through three years of the French Revolution, and many other dreams of the same nature, are instances of this. Now, Fechner has proved, in his *Elemente der Psychophysik*, first, that a fraction of a second is needed for the sensorial contact to cause the brain to vibrate—this prevents our perceiving the growth of a plant and enables us to see a circle of fire when a piece of glowing coal is rapidly whirled round; secondly, that another fraction of a second is needed for the cerebral vibration to be transformed into sensation. We might add that a third fraction of a second is needed for sensation to be transformed into ideation, proving that in these special dreams there can have been no more than an instantaneous, mass impression of all the elements of the dream upon the brain,[7] and that the dream itself has been produced by the imaginative action of the soul in the astral body, an extremely subtle one, whose vibratory power is such as to transform altogether our ordinary notions of time and space.

The death-bed dream. In dying people, the bodily senses gradually lose their vitality, and by degrees the soul concentrates itself within the finer vehicle. From that time signs of the higher consciousness appear, time is inordinately prolonged, visions present themselves, the prophetic faculty is sometimes manifested, and verified cases are related of removal to a distance, like that of the Alsatian woman dying on board ship. During the final coma she went to Rio de Janeiro and commended her child to the keeping of a fellow-countryman. (D'Assier's *L'humanite posthume*, p. 47) Similar instances are found in *The Night Side of Nature*, by C. Crowe, as well as in other works of the same kind.

The dream of intoxication. Under the influence of soporifics the same transfer of consciousness is produced, and we meet with more or less remarkable phenomena due to the higher consciousness. Opium smokers and eaters of hashish are able to form ideas with such rapidity that minutes seem to them to be years, and a few moments in dreamland delude them into the idea that they have lived through a whole life. (Hervey's *Les reves et les moyens de les diriger.*)

The dream of asphyxia. During asphyxia by submersion the higher consciousness enters into a minute study of the life now running to its close. In a few moments it sees the whole of it again in its smallest details. Carl du Prel (*Philos. der Mystik*) gives several instances of this; Haddock (*Somnolism and Psychism*, p. 213) quotes, among other cases, that of Admiral Beaufort. During two minutes' loss of consciousness in a drowning condition, he saw again every detail of his life, all his actions, including their causes, collateral circumstances, their effects, and the reflections of the victim on the good and evil that had resulted therefrom.

Perty's account (*Die Mystischen Erscheinungen der Menschlichen Natur*) of Catherine Emmerich, the somnambulist nun, who, when dying, saw again the whole of her past life, would incline one to think that this strange phenomenon, which traditional Catholicism appears to have called the "Private Judgment," and which theosophy defines with greater preciseness, is not limited to asphyxia by submersion, but is the regular accompaniment of life's ending.

MANIFESTATION OF THE HIGHER CONSCIOUSNESS IN VARIOUS CASES OF MENTAL FACULTIES LOST TO NORMAL CONSCIOUSNESS

A rather large number of people born blind have images in dreams, and can see with the higher consciousness, when placed in a state of somnambulism. This proves that the higher consciousness possesses the power of vision on its own plane, and can impress images thereof on the brain.

That this impression may be translated into the language of the physical plane,[8] it must evidently take place in one of the physical centres of vision which make possible three-dimensional sight; these centres may be intact even when the external visual apparatus does not exist or is incapable of functioning.

A deaf and dumb idiot became intelligent and spoke during spontaneous somnambulism (Steinbach's *Der Dichter ein Seher*). This is a case which appears to us difficult to explain fully; indeed, if the impression of the higher vibration on that portion of the brain which presides over intelligence and thought can be understood, it is not easy to see how tongue and lips could suddenly utter precise sounds which they had never produced before. Another factor must have intervened here, as was the case with the child prophets of the Camisards. (V. Figuier's *Hist. du merveilleux, etc.*)

Young Hebert, who had gone mad as the result of a wound, regained full consciousness, the higher consciousness, during somnambulism. (Puysegur's *Journal du traitement du jeune Hebert.*)

Dr. Teste (*Manuel pratiq. du magnet. anim.*) came across madmen who became sane just before death, *i.e.*, when consciousness was passing into the astral body. He also mentions a servant girl, quite uneducated and of ordinary intelligence, who nevertheless became a veritable philosopher during mesmeric somnambulism and delivered learned discourses on lofty problems dealing with cosmogony.

This proves that the vibratory scale of the finer vehicle extends far beyond that of the physical, and that the soul cannot impress on this latter vehicle all that it knows when functioning in the former. By this we do not mean that it is omniscient as soon as it has left the visible body; this opinion, a current one, is contrary to the law of evolution, and will not bear examination.

MANIFESTATIONS OF THE HIGHER CONSCIOUSNESS UNDER THE FORM OF MEMORY

The memory that is lost by the brain is preserved in its entirety by the finer vehicle.

A musician, a friend of Hervey's, once heard a remarkable piece of music; he remembered it on awaking, and wrote it down, regarding it as his own inspiration. Many years afterwards, he found it in an old parcel of music where he knew it had been long before; he had totally forgotten it in his normal consciousness. (Hervey's *Dreams.*)

Coleridge tells of a servant girl who, when in a state of delirium, would recite long passages of Hebrew which she had formerly heard from the lips of a priest in whose service she had been. In the same way, she would repeat passages from Latin and Greek theological books, which she had heard under the same circumstances; in her normal state, she had no recollection whatever of all this. (Dr. Carpenter's *Mental Physiology*, p. 437, 1881 edition.)

Ricard (*Physiol. et Hygiene du Magnet.*, p. 183) relates the case of a young man, possessed of an ordinary memory, but who, in somnambulism, could repeat almost word for word a sermon he had heard or a book he had read.

Mayo, the physiologist, states that an ignorant young girl, in a state of somnambulism, wrote whole pages of a treatise on astronomy, including figures and calculations, which she had probably read in the *Encyclopaedia Britannica*, for the treatise was afterwards found in that work. (*Truths in Popular Superstitions.*)

Ladame (*La Nevrose hypnotique*, p. 105) mentions a woman who, having only on one occasion been to the theatre, was able, during somnambulism, to sing the whole of the second act of Meyerbeer's *L'Africaine*, an opera of which she knew nothing whatever in her waking state.

During experiments with the inhaling of protoxyde of azote, H. Davy said that normal consciousness disappeared, and was followed by a wonderful power of recalling past events. (Hibbert's *Philosophy of Apparitions*, p. 162.)

MANIFESTATIONS OF THE HIGHER CONSCIOUSNESS IN PHENOMENA OF DOUBLE CONSCIOUSNESS

The "strata of memory" met with in many cases also prove the existence of the second vehicle of consciousness which we are trying to demonstrate.

Certain dreams continue night after night, beginning again just where they stopped the previous night; this is noticed in the case of those who talk in their sleep and in spontaneous or forced somnambulism.

The memory of one intoxicated, or in a state of fever delirium is lost when consciousness returns from the astral to the physical body; it comes back on the return of the delirium or the intoxication.

The same thing takes place in madness; at the termination of a crisis, the patients take up the past just where they left it. (Wienholt's *Heilkraft*.) Kerner relates that one of these unfortunate persons, after an illness lasting several years, remembered the last thing he did before the crisis happened, his first question being whether the tools with which he had been cutting up wood had been put away. During the whole of the interval he had been living in his higher consciousness.

Ribot (*Maladies de la Memoire* p. 63) has noted the fact that the same thing happens with those who fall into a state of coma after having received a hurt or wound.

MANIFESTATIONS OF THE HIGHER CONSCIOUSNESS, INDICATING NOT ONLY THAT IT EXTENDS FARTHER THAN NORMAL CONSCIOUSNESS, BUT DOMINATES, AND IS SEPARATED FROM IT, RECOGNISING THAT ITS VEHICLE—THE BODY— IS NOTHING MORE THAN AN INSTRUMENT

The Soul functioning in the finer body sees the physical body in a state of coma. Dr. Abercrombie relates the case of a child aged four, who was trepanned as the result of fracture of the skull, and whilst in a stale of coma. He never knew what happened. At the age of fifteen, during an attack of fever, the higher consciousness impressed itself upon the brain, and he remembered every detail of the accident; he described to his mother where he had felt the pain, the operation, the people present, their number, functions, the clothes they wore, the instruments used, etc. (Kerner, *Magikon*, vol. 3, p. 364.)

The Soul, in the finer body, during somnambulism, is separated both from the physical body and from normal consciousness, it calmly foresees the illness or the death of the denser body on which it sometimes imposes serious operations. Such facts were numerous in the case of magnetisers in olden days.

Deleuze (*Hist. crit. du magn. animal*, vol. 2, p. 173) had a patient who, in a state of somnambulism, held moral, philosophical, and religious opinions quite contrary to those of his waking state.

Charpignon (*Physiol., medecine et metaphys. du magnetisme*, p. 341) tells of a patient who, when awake, wished to go to the theatre, but during somnambulism refused to do so, saying:

"*She* wants to go, but *I* don't want." On Charpignon recommending that she should try to turn *her* aside from her purpose, she replied: "What can I do? *She* is mad!"

Deleuze (*Inst. pratiq. s. le maget. anim.*, p. 121) says that many somnambulists look into their body when the latter is ill; that they are often indifferent to its sufferings, and sometimes are not even willing to prescribe remedies to cure it.

Chardel (*Esquisse de la nat. humaine expliq. p. le magn. anim.*, p. 282) relates that many somnambulists are unwilling to be awakened so as not to return to a body which is a hindrance to them.

There are many madmen who speak of their body in the third person. (Ladame, *La Nevrose*, p. 43). They function in the non-externalised finer vehicle. Some explain their use of the third person as follows:—"*It* is the body; it is *I* who am the spirit."

MANIFESTATION OF THE HIGHER CONSCIOUSNESS IN THE PHENOMENA OF POSSESSION AND MATERIALISATION

In these strange phenomena, not only manifestations of the higher consciousness, analogous with or similar to those just cited, have been noted, but also a number of facts which prove, to some extent, the casual presence in a normal human body or in materialised abnormal forms, of beings other than that which constitutes the personality of the one possessed, or of the medium who conditions these materialisations. On this point, we would mention the well-known investigations of Sir W. Crookes (*Katie King*), those of Colonel de Rochas (Vincent, *Un cas de changement de personnalite, Lotus Bleu* 1896), and similar experiments of other savants.

"Incarnation mediums" have often lent their physical bodies to disincarnated human entities, whose account of what happened or whose identity it has been possible to verify. Here I will mention only one case amongst several others, I heard it from my friend, D. A. Courmes, a retired naval captain, a man who is well-informed in these matters, thoroughly sincere, and of unquestioned veracity.

In 1895, he happened to be off Algiers, on a training vessel. A boat had sunk in the harbour, and a man was drowned. His body had not been recovered. On the evening of the accident, my friend, accompanied by a doctor, a professor, and the vice-president of the Court of Algiers, attended a spiritualistic meeting in the town. One of these "incarnation mediums" happened to be present. M. Courmes suggested that the drowned man should be called up. The latter answered to the call, entered the medium, whose voice and attitude immediately changed. He gave the following account of what had taken place: "When the boat sank, I was on the ladder. I was hurled down, my right leg passed between two bars, occasioning fracture of the leg, and preventing me from releasing myself. My body will be found caught in the ladder when the boat is brought to the surface. It is useless to seek elsewhere."

This account was shortly afterwards confirmed.

These phenomena are more frequent than one would imagine; a sufficient number might be given to show that, judging from the theory of probabilities, serious consideration should be given to them.

MANIFESTATIONS OF THE HIGHER
CONSCIOUSNESS IN APPARITIONS

A final group of phenomena to which I wish to call attention is the one which goes under the name of apparitions. A considerable number of these are to be found; we will confine ourselves, however, to referring the reader to a volume entitled *Phantasms of the Living*, due to the patient investigations of a distinguished body of foreign savants. Here we find, first of all, proof of the transmission of thought to a distance. An examination into the conditions under which most of these cases took place has convinced several students of the existence of the finer body which we are here endeavouring to demonstrate, as well as of the possibility of its instantaneous transference to a great distance. As the proofs afforded by apparitions are not mathematical, *i.e.*, indisputable, and as they give room for a variety of opinions, we will make no attempt to detail them, preferring to pass on to a final proof—the least important, perhaps, from a general point of view, since it is limited to the individual possessing it; the only absolute and mathematical one, however, to the man who has obtained it:—the personal proof.

There are persons—few in number, true—who, under divers influences, have been able to leave the physical body and see it sleeping on a couch. They have freely moved in an environment—the astral world—similar to our physical one in some respects, though different in many others, and have returned again to the body, bringing back the memory of their wanderings. These accounts have been given by persons deserving of credence and not subject to hallucinations.

There are other individuals, though not so numerous—of whom we have the pleasure of knowing some personally—who are able to leave their physical bodies and return at will.

They travel to great distances with the utmost rapidity and bring back a complete memory of their journeyings. D'Assier gives a typical case in his work. (*L'Humanite posthume*, p. 59.)

Such is the proof we look upon as irrefutable, as complete and perfect. The man who can thus travel freely in his finer body knows that the physical body is only a vehicle adapted to the physical world and necessary for life in this world; he knows that consciousness does not cease to function, and that the universe by no means provides the conditions for a state of nothingness, once this body of flesh is laid aside.

At this stage of his evolution man can, in addition, make use of his astral body at will, and obtain on the astral plane, first by reason and intuition, afterwards by personal experience, proof of another vehicle of consciousness—the mental body. At a further stage he obtains the certainty of possession of the causal body, then of higher bodies, and from that time he can no longer doubt the teachings of the Elder Brothers, those who have entered the higher evolution, the worlds that are divine. He knows, beyond all possibility of doubt, that what the ordinary man expresses in such childish language regarding these lofty problems, what he calls the Absolute and the Manifested, God and the Universe, the soul and the body, are more vitally true than he imagined; he sees that these words are dense veils that conceal the supreme, ineffable, infinite Being, of whom manifested beings are illusory "aspects," facets of the divine Jewel.[9]

With this introduction, we will plunge at once into the heart of the subject.

FOOTNOTES:

[Footnote 2: Which is nothing but an unknown "aspect" of

abstract Divinity.]

[Footnote 3: Present-day man possesses four bodies of increasing fineness, the elements of which interpenetrate. Proceeding from the most dense, these are: The physical, the astral, the mental, and the causal body. In certain conditions they are capable of dissociation, and they last for a longer or a shorter time. The astral body, also called the body of desire, animal soul (Kamarupa, in Sanskrit) is the seat of sensation. Evolution has in store for us higher bodies stilt— the buddhic body, the atmic body, &c.... but these need only be mentioned at this point.

Yoga—Sanskrit, *union*—is a training of the different bodies of man by the will; its object is to make of those bodies complete and perfect instruments, capable of responding to the vibrations of the outer universe as well as to those of the individual soul. When this process is accomplished, man can receive, consciously and at will, in any one of his bodies, vibrations received by the soul primarily in one of the others; for instance, he may feel in the physical brain the direct action of his astral or higher bodies; he may also leave the physical, and feel directly in his astral body the action of the mental body, and so on.

Yoga can be practised only under the guidance of a Master, *i.e.*, a highly developed being, capable of guiding the student safely through the dangers incidental to this training.]

[Footnote 4: When the astral body is externalised, the subject cannot speak; he must await its return; when only partially externalised or not at all, and consciousness is centred in it, the subject can speak and relate what he sees afar off, for astral vision is possible at enormous distances. Such cases as these are frequently met with.]

[Footnote 5: In 1876, in a Leipzic hospital, there was a patient possessed of neither sensibility nor muscular sense. He had only sight in the right eye and hearing in the left ear. If this eye and ear were closed, the patient immediately fell asleep. Neither by being touched nor shaken could he be awakened; to effect this, it was necessary to open his eye and unstop his ear. (*Archiv. fuer die ges. Physiologie*, vol. 15, p. 573).]

[Footnote 6: These pictures are often visible in the astral world; they explain the prophetic faculty of ordinary seers.]

[Footnote 7: In such cases, by association of ideas or any other influence, the soul dramatises the physical impression which calls forth the dream, and creates the long phantasmagoria of this dream in so short a time as to be scarcely appreciable. Between the sleeping physical body and the externalised astral body there is so close a degree of sympathy that the latter is conscious of everything that takes place in the former. This explains why the astral body returns so rapidly to the physical when a noise, light, or any other sensation impresses this latter.]

[Footnote 8: We say "language of the physical plane" because the soul, in the astral body, sees in four dimensions, *i.e.*, all the parts of an object at once, as though these parts were spread out on a two-dimensional plane. Consequently, the higher vision needs interpretation in order to be expressed on the physical plane.]

[Footnote 9: There are other proofs of the existence of the causal body, the reincarnating vehicle; the principal one is given in the middle of Chapter 3. It is there shown that the physical germs explain only a very small portion of heredity, and that logic imperiously demands the existence of an invisible, durable body, capable of gathering up the germs which preserve the moral and intellectual qualities of man.]

Th. Pascal

CHAPTER II

REINCARNATION AND THE MORAL LAW

The Goodness, justice, and Omnipotence of God are the guarantees of Providence.

It is absolutely impossible that the faintest breath of injustice should ever disturb the Universe. Every time the Law appears to be violated, every time Justice seems outraged, we may be certain that it is our ignorance alone that is at work, and that a deeper knowledge of the net-work of evolution and of the lines of action created by human free will, sooner or later, will dissipate our error.

For all that, the whole universe appears to be the very incarnation of injustice. The constellations as they come into manifestation shatter the heavens with their titanic combats; it is the vampirism of the greatest among them that creates the suns, thus inaugurating egoism from the very beginning. Everywhere on earth is heard the cry of pain, a never-ending struggle; sacrifice is everywhere, whether voluntary or forced, offered freely or taken unwillingly. The law of the strongest is the universal tyranny. The vegetable kingdom feeds upon the mineral, and in its turn forms nourishment for the animal; the giants of the forests spread ruin in every direction, beneath their destructive influence the spent, exhausted soil can nourish nothing but weeds and shrubs of no importance. In the animal kingdom a war to the death is ever being waged, a terrible destruction in which those best armed for the fray pitilessly devour the weak and defenceless. Man piles up every kind and method of destruction, cruelty and barbarity of every sort; he tears away gold from the bowels of the earth, mutilates the mighty forests, exhausts the soil by intensive culture, harasses and tortures animals when unable to utilise their muscular strength, and, in addition, kills them when their flesh is eatable; his most careful calculations are the auxiliaries of his insatiable egoism, and, by might or cunning, he crushes everything that hinders or inconveniences him. Finally, from time to time, the Elements mingle their awful voice in this concert of pain and despair, and we find hurricanes and floods, fires and earthquakes pile up colossal wreck and ruin in a few hours, on which scenes of destruction the morrow's calm and glorious sun sheds his impassive beams.

And so, before reaching individual evil and apparent injustice, there rises up before us at the very outset the threatening spectre of universal evil and injustice. This problem is so closely bound up with our subject that we are compelled to spend a short time in considering it.

WHY DOES PAIN EXIST?

To admit, as do certain ignorant fatalists, that the Universe was created by the stroke of some magic wand, and that each planet, kingdom, and being is condemned, so to speak, to a definite crystallisation in the state in which it has pleased God to fix it; to admit that the mineral will remain a mineral throughout eternity, that the vegetable will ever reproduce the same types, that the animal will definitely be confined to

Th. Pascal

his instincts and impulses, without the hope, some day, of developing the superior mentality of his torturers in human form; to admit that man will never be anything but man, *i.e.*, a being in whom the passions have full play whereas the virtues are scarcely born; to admit that there is no final goal—perfection, the divine state—to crown man's labour; all this is to refuse to recognise evolution, to deny the progress everywhere apparent, to set divine below human justice; blasphemy, in a word.

It has been said by unthinking Christians that evidently God created human suffering, so that those might gain Heaven who, but for this suffering, would have no right to it. To speak thus is to represent the Supreme Goodness in a very unworthy aspect and to attribute the most gratuitous cruelty to Divine Justice. When, too, we see that this absurd reasoning explains neither the sufferings of animals, which have no right to enjoy the felicity of heaven, they say, nor the fact[10] that "there are many called but few chosen," nor the saying that "outside the Church there is no salvation," although for ages past God has caused millions of men to be born in countries where the Gospel has not been preached, we shall not be astonished to find that those who arrogate to themselves a monopoly of Truth bring forward none but arguments of childish folly in support of their claims.

Generally, however, it is original sin that is advanced as the cause of suffering.

The absurdity of this doctrine is so apparent that it has lost all credence by enlightened members of the Christian faith. First of all, it does not explain the sufferings of animals, which have had no participation in this sin, nor does it account for the unequal distribution of pain amongst men themselves. This sin being the same for all at birth,[11] punishment ought to have been equally severe for all, and we ought not to see such frightful disproportions as are to be found in the condition of children who have not attained to the age of reason, *i.e.*, of responsibility. Saint Augustine felt the weight of this consideration; he reflected long on this torturing problem:

"When I come to consider the sufferings of children," he says, "believe me, I am in a state of terrible perplexity. I have no wish whatever to speak only of the punishment inflicted on them after this life by eternal damnation to which they are of necessity condemned if they have left their bodies without receiving the sacrament of Christ, but of the pains they endure in this present life, under our very eyes. Did I wish to examine these sufferings, time would fail me rather than instances thereof; they languish in sickness, are torn by pain, tortured by hunger and thirst, weakened in their organs, deprived of their senses, and sometimes tormented by unclean beings. I should have to show how they can with justice be subjected to such things, at a time when they are yet without sin. It cannot be said that they suffer unknown to God or that God can do nothing against their tormentors, nor that He can create or allow unjust punishment. When men suffer, we say they are being punished for their crimes, but this can be applied only to adults. As children have in them no sin capable of meriting so terrible a punishment, tell me what answer can be given?"

The answer, indeed, cannot be made that original sin is capable of explaining this unequal retribution; but then, ought not the very absurdity of the consequences due to such sin to justify one in refusing to examine this argument? What soul could admit that the innocent should be punished for the guilty? Does human justice, in spite of its imperfection, punish the offspring of criminals? Can the millions of descendants of the mythical Adam have been chastised for a crime in which they have had no share? And would this chastisement, multiplied millions of times without the faintest reason, never have stirred the conscience of the Church? Saint Augustine could not make up his mind to accuse God of injustice; so, to avoid disputing the truth of the Christian teaching in which he wholly believed, he invented his famous theory of "generation," often called "translation."

Men suffer because of original sin, he says, but it would not be just of God to punish them for this, had they not shared therein[12]; this, indeed, they have done, for the soul of a man was not created directly, by God, at the moment of the birth of the body; it is a branch taken from the soul of his father, as the latter's comes from that of his parents; thus, ascending the genealogical chain, we see that all souls issue from that of the common father of mankind: Adam.[13]

So that Saint Augustine preferred to deny the creation of souls and to derive them from the soul of Adam, through a successive progeny of human vehicles, rather than to allow God to be charged with injustice. We are not called upon to demonstrate the falsity of his hypothesis, which the Church has been forced to condemn, though without replacing it with a better theory; all the same, if human souls suffer from a sin in which they have not individually and consciously participated—and such is the case, for even granting that translation be a fact, these souls existed in Adam only potentially, as unconscious, undeveloped germs, when the sin took place—their punishment is none the less arbitrary and revolting. Saint Augustine believed he was justifying Providence; he succeeded only in deceiving his own reason and revolted sense of justice, but he preferred by suggestion to deceive himself to such an extent as to believe in the reality of his desire rather than enrol himself against the Church.

In order to reconcile divine Justice with the injustice of punishing all for the fault of one alone, the theologians also said: "Adam sinned, his sin has been distributed over the whole of his race, but God, by sending down his son, instituted baptism; and the waters of the sacrament wash the stains of original sin from the souls of men."

This reply is as childish as the former. As a matter of fact, according to the Church, about four thousand years intervened between the sin of Adam and the coming of the Redeemer, and so only after that interval did the souls of the just, who were waiting in the Life Beyond for the coming of the Messiah, enter Paradise!

Would not this delay in itself be an injustice? Ought not baptism to have been instituted immediately after the sin, and should it not have been placed within the reach of all? Besides, do we not see that even in our days, two thousand years after the coming of the Christ, millions of human beings are born and die without ever having heard of the existence of this sacrament. This part of the argument is too puerile to dwell upon at length, but we will spend a few moments on it to show definitely how powerless this theory is to explain evil.

Before teaching the doctrine of "Limbo," the Church accepted the idea of the damnation of children who died without being baptised, as we have just seen in the case of Saint Augustine.[14] Bossuet, with incredible blindness, also accepted it; and, sad to relate, his reason did not feel called upon to furnish an explanation which would justify Providence, as was the case with Saint Augustine. He rejected "translation," and discovered nothing with which to veil the blasphemy.

On this point the following is a faithful *resume* of his letter to Pope Innocent XII.:

> The damnation of children who have died without being baptised must be firmly believed by the Church. They are guilty because they are born under the wrath of God and in the power of Darkness. Children of wrath by nature, objects of hatred and aversion, hurled into Hell with the rest of the damned, they will remain there for all eternity punished by the horrible vengeance of the Demon.

> Such also are the decisions of the learned Denis Petau, the most eminent Bellarmin, the Councils of Lyons, of Florence, and of Trent; for these things are not decided by human considerations, but by the authority of tradition and of the Scriptures.

Such logic makes one really doubt human reason, and reminds one of the spirit with which the courts of the Holy Inquisition were inspired. Where in Nature can there be found such lack of proportion between cause and effect, crime and punishment? Have such arguments ever been justified by the voice of conscience?

Official Christianity remains powerless to explain suffering. Let us see what we can learn from the philosophies and religions of the past and the greatest of modern philosophers, as well as from the admirable *resumes* of Teachers of theosophy.

The problem of suffering is one with that of life, *i.e.*, with that of evolution in general. The object of the successive worlds is the creation of millions of centres of consciousness in the germinal state (*souls*) and the transformation of these germs into divinities similar to their father, God. This is the divine multiplication, creating innumerable "gods," in God.

To produce divine germs, homogeneous Unity must limit its immensity and create within itself the diversity of matter, of form. This can be obtained by the creation of "multiplicity" and by the "limitation" of what might be called a portion of Divinity. Now, limitation implies imperfection, both general and individual, *i.e.*, suffering; and multiplicity implies diversity of needs and interests, forced submission to the general law *i.e.*, suffering again. That the divine germs may evolve, their potentialities must be awakened by their surroundings; in other words, by the action of the "opposites," and sensation must come into being; the action of the opposites on sensation is also a cause of pain.

Outside of the unknown Being—which will be known at the end of evolution—nothing can *be*. Everything is in Him. He is all; the worlds, time and space are "aspects" which He assumes from time to time[15]; for this reason it has been said that the Universe is an illusion, which may be expressed more clearly by saying that it is an illusion to believe that what exists is not one form of divine activity, an "aspect" of God.

That anything may exist, or rather that aspects of God may appear, there must be manifested in Him a special mode of being, to call forth what we designate as multiplicity.

That multiplicity[16] may be manifest, differences must be produced in Unity; these differences in the world are the "pairs of opposites"—the contraries. These contraries are everywhere.

Matter is the fulcrum of force—both of these terms being "aspects" of God—and without a fulcrum no force can manifest itself; there is no heat without cold, and when it is summer in the northern hemisphere it is winter in the southern. There is no movement that does not depend upon a state of rest, no light without shadow, no pleasure without the faculty of pain, no freedom that is not founded upon necessity, no good that does not betoken an evil.

The following are a few examples of duality taken from nature. The current of electricity is polarised into a positive and a negative current. It is the same with the magnet; though you break a bar into a hundred pieces, you bring into being a hundred small magnets, each possessing its positive and negative side; you will not have destroyed the "duality," the opposites.

Like the magnet, the solar spectrum forms two series, separated by a neutral point, the blue series and the red one, united by the violet.[17]

Violet.

Indigo.	Yellow.
Blue.	Orange.
Green.	Red.

The terms of the two series are respectively complimentary to each other; the violet dominates the two groups of opposites and is a visible member of the axis formed by the colours that might be called neutral.

Duality appears in every shape and form.

Symbolically, we may say with the Hindus that the Universe begins and ends with two opposite movements: an emanation from Brahma, it is born when the breast of God sends forth the heavenly outbreathing, it dies, reabsorbed, when the universal inbreathing takes place. These movements produce attraction and repulsion, the aggregation and dissolution to be found everywhere. It is the attraction of a force-centre, the "laya centre" of Theosophy, which permits of the atomic condensation that gives it the envelope whose soul it is; when its cycle of activity ends, attraction gives place to repulsion, the envelope is destroyed by the return of its constituent elements to the source from which they were drawn, and the soul is liberated until a future cycle of activity begins.

Even the rhythm of pulmonary respiration, the contraction and dilation (systole and diastole) of the heart, the ebb and flow of the tides, as also day and night, sleeping and waking, summer and winter, life and death, are all products of that law of contraries which rules creation.

These "opposites" are the very essence of cosmic life, the twin pillars of universal equilibrium; they have been represented in Solomon's symbolical temple—here, the Universe—by Jakin and Boaz, the white and the black columns; they are also the interlaced triangles of "Solomon's Seal," the six-pointed star, the two Old Men of the Kabbalah, the white Jehovah and the black Jehovah; Eros and Anteros, the serpents of Mercury's caduceus, the two Sphinxes of the car of Osiris, Adam and Eve, Cain and Abel, Jacob and Esau, the Chinese "Yang" and "Yin," the goblet and staff of Tarot, man and woman. All these images represent the same law.

Multiplicity, the fruit of the contraries, makes its appearance in the forms born in infinite, homogeneous Being; its goal is the goal of creation; the production, in infinite Being, of centres which are developed by evolution and finally become gods in God. These centres, or "souls," these points in the supreme Point, are divine in essence, though, so far, they have no share at all in the perfection "manifested" by God; they are all "centres," for God is a sphere, whose centre is everywhere and circumference nowhere, but they have not developed consciousness which is as yet only potential in them. Like cuttings of willow which reproduce the mother-tree, these points, veritable portions of God, are capable of germinating, growing up, and becoming "I's," self-conscious beings, intelligent and endowed with will-power, and finally gods, having developed the entire potentialities of the All by their repeated imprisonment in the series of forms that make up the visible and invisible kingdoms of nature.

Every form, *i.e.* aggregate of substance-force, reflects within itself one of these points of Divinity. This point is its Monad, its centre of consciousness, or soul; it is the cause which is manifested as qualities in the envelopes, and these give it the illusion of separateness for a certain period,[18] just as a soap-bubble momentarily acquires a fictitious individuality and appears separate from the atmosphere—of which it forms part—so long as its illusory envelope endures.

Thus do men imagine themselves separate from one another, when all the time their soul is nothing more than a drop of the divine Ocean, hidden momentarily in a perishable body.

The "contraries" are the anvil and the hammer which slowly forge souls by producing what might be called sensation in general, and sensation is a fertile cause of suffering each time the vehicles of consciousness receive vibrations that greatly exceed their fundamental capacity of sensation. Without sensation however—consequently without suffering —the body could neither walk,[19] nor see, nor hear, nor show any disturbance brought to bear upon it; there would exist no possible relation between the Universe and the "I," between the All and the parts, between bodies and souls; there would be no consciousness, or sensation of being, since no vibration from without would find an echo in the incarnated "centres" of life; no knowledge would be possible; man would be, as it were, in a state of nothingness; and, without suspecting it, his body might at any moment be crushed to the ground by the forces of Nature.

But these material necessities are not by any means the only ones that demand sensation; without it, one of the principal objects of evolution—the development of "Egos"—would be impossible. As an example borrowed from the domain of physical sensation, we need only call to memory a well-known experience in childhood.

All who have been at a boarding school know how heavy and fetid is the atmosphere of a dormitory in the early winter morning, when fifty boys have been breathing the same air again and again during the whole of the night. And yet, who suspected this until he had gone out for a few minutes and then returned to the bed-room? It needed the "contrary," the pure outside air, to make known the state of the atmosphere inside. The contrast produced sensation—that nauseous, suffocating impression of foul, mephitic air; suffering[20] generated knowledge of the vitiated air; as the result of this influence, the "centre of consciousness" felt itself an "I" distinct from its surroundings, and its "self-consciousness" received a slight increase.

What might be called passional sensibility—desire, emotion, impulse—is, like physical sensation, another indispensable factor in evolution; it is the special element in the development of the animal kingdom as well as of the less evolved portion of the human kingdom.

The young souls of mankind must receive the comparatively simple lessons of sensation, desire, and passion, before begin-ning the far more complicated study of mentality. But for desire, a host of needs could not be manifested, numberless functions would remain inactive; the body would not feed itself, and would die, were it not for hunger; danger would not be fled from, but for the instinct of self-preservation; nor without this would there be any propagation of the species. None the less is this life of sensation the source of many evils; desire and passion amongst human beings create terrible misery, fill prisons and hospitals, and are at the root of all kinds of moral suffering. In its turn, intelligence—that sensation so characteristic of the human state—is both an indispensable necessity and the most fertile source of evil, so long as it has not experienced a yearning for that inner "divinity," deep in the heart of man, which calls to it. A powerful lever of progress, it might convert this earth into a paradise, whereas it is the weapon which the strong, in their egoism, use to crush the feeble, a terrible weapon which either creates or intensifies all the evils under which the people writhe in despair. Once it becomes the instrument of a regenerate humanity, that is to say, when men have become compassionate, loving, and devoted, then the social question will cease to exist, and the old instrument of torture will become a pledge of general happiness.

Even spiritual sensibility is a cause of suffering to some noble souls who have developed it, for however deep the joy of loving and giving oneself, intense too is the pain of witnessing the cruel drama of life, that fratricidal struggle in which passion strikes without mercy, whilst illusion and ignorance deal blows even more terrible, for into the wounds they make they instil the poison of revolt and despair.

The action of multiplicity, and of its creators, the "contraries," engenders still other causes of suffering. Every being lives both for others and at their expense. For instance, physical bodies are obliged to replace with food and nourishment those particles which the various functions of life cause them to lose. The vegetable kingdom takes its constituent elements from the mineral kingdom, and itself serves as food for large portions of the animal kingdom; up to this point physical pain has not manifested itself, though there is a momentary arrest of evolution for the animistic essence which represents the individual in the destroyed vegetable. A portion of the animal kingdom feeds on its own members; man, too, extorts from this same kingdom a very heavy tribute; here, the arrested evolution of the victims is all the more important, inasmuch as their stage of evolution is higher, and the existence of a nervous system brings the possibility of suffering, suffering which certain influences[21] either diminish or suppress altogether, when caused by animal destructiveness, but which may become intense when it is man who is the sacrificer.

Among the causes of pain, arising from multiplicity there is also the physical, mental, and moral action exercised by the solidarity of all beings. By exchanging, with those that come into contact with us, the products thrown off by our visible and invisible bodies, we are the dispensers of good or ill-health. Everyone, for instance, is aware of the far-reaching effects of an evil intellectual and moral example; physical contagion, in spite of the torture it inflicts, is far less to be dreaded than moral contagion. The spiritual qualities alone do not form a leaven of evil; they are not the double-edged instruments we meet with elsewhere. The reason of this is that they belong to the plane of Unity. But it is none the less true that, though the presence of a highly developed soul is a help to younger souls within its reach and influence, its powerful vibrations may, from certain points of view, prove fatiguing to those still at the foot of the ladder of evolution. This is one of the many reasons that have given rise to the saying that it is dangerous prematurely to enter the "circle of the ascetics."

But the most powerful causes of pain, due to multiplicity, are the ignorance and the will of beings who have reached the human stage. Man can employ his mental faculties for good or evil, and so long as he does not know definitely that he is the brother of all beings, *i.e.*, until his divine faculties have been developed, and love and the spirit of sacrifice have taken possession of his heart, he remains a terrible egoist, more to be dreaded than the criminal dominated by a momentary burst of passion, for he acts in cold blood, he evades or refuses to recognise the law of humanity, he dominates and destroys. This man is at the stage of ingratitude; he no longer possesses the harmlessness of childhood, nor has he yet acquired the wisdom of advanced age. Our Western race has reached this critical stage, whereof the menacing demands of the suffering masses are a striking testimony. Here, too, God could not do otherwise; He might create bodies blindly obedient to his law, mere automata, but it would be impossible for Him to cause divine germs to evolve into "gods" without pulling them through the school of evolution which teaches them, first, of the "ego," the root of all egoism, then knowledge by ignorance, liberty by necessity, good by evil, and the perfect by the imperfect.

It may at this point just be mentioned that though human egoism appears to have free play and to be unrestrained in its cruelty, divine Law never allows innocence to suffer for the errors of evolving souls, it punishes only the guilty, whether their faults or misdeeds be known or unknown, belonging to the present life or to past ones.

Such, briefly, is the cause of pain and suffering in evolution; in the following pages we will set forth the causes of the unequal distribution of this suffering.

THE PROBLEM OF THE INEQUALITY OF CONDITIONS

If suffering in general is the child of Necessity—since it is born of multiplicity and the limitation of the Infinite, without which the Universe could not exist—it would seem that we ought to find it falling upon all beings without distinction, in uniform, regular, and impartial fashion. Instead of this, it is every moment losing its character of impersonality; it respects those who are guilty on a large scale; and, without any visible cause, strikes fiercely the most innocent of persons; noble souls are born in the families of criminals, whilst criminals have fathers of the utmost respectability; we find parricides, and brothers hostile to each other; millionaires die of surfeiting alongside of paupers dying of hunger; we find giants by the side of dwarfs; the healthy and well-formed near the crippled or those wasted away by terrible diseases; Apollos contrast with Quasimodos; men of genius are met with, cheek by jowl with idiots; some children are stillborn, others blind or deaf and dumb from birth. Extremely different races people the earth—on the one hand, unintelligent and cannibal negroes; on the other, the proud, handsome, and intelligent, though selfish and cruel white race. Again, from a moral standpoint, who can explain congenital tendencies to crime, the vicious by birth, the wicked by nature, the persons with uncontrollable passions? Wherefore are thrift and foresight lacking in so many men, who are consequently condemned to lifelong poverty and wretchedness? Why this excess of intelligence, used mainly for the exploiting of folly? It is useless to multiply examples, one has only to look around at hospitals and prisons, night-shelters, palaces and garrets; everywhere suffering has taken up its abode. Can no reply be given to this terrible charge brought against Divinity? Is man to remain in a state of dejection and discouragement, as though some irreparable catastrophe had befallen him?

According to the Church, all this is the work of the soul which God gives at the birth of a man—a soul that is good or bad, prudent or foolish, one which damns or saves itself according as its will can, or cannot, dominate its passions, its intelligence discover the way to heaven or not; according as grace or rejection predestine it to heaven or to hell.

Is it not the depth of profanity to represent God as watching over conceptions in order to create souls so unfairly endowed, most of whom will never hear the Gospel message, and consequently cannot be saved, whilst the rest are destined to animate the bodies of savages and cannibals, devoid of moral consciousness? Is it not an act of sacrilege thus to convert God, Who is all Wisdom and Love, into a kind of accomplice of adulterers and lewd persons or the sport of Malthusian insults. Unconscious blasphemers are they who would offer this Dead Sea fruit as the true manna of Life!

There is also another theory, often advanced in certain quarters, on which we must say a few words, for though it contains only a minimum of truth, and consequently cannot withstand serious examination, it has led astray more than one earnest thinker. Inequalities of suffering, it has been said, arise from inequalities of social conditions. Intelligence, morality, will, in fact all human faculties, develop more or less according to their environment; men are born equal; they become unequal as the result of different environment; pay the same care and attention to all and they will remain equal, and if they are equal, the theory seems to imply, evil will disappear from the face of the earth.

This is not so.

Inequality of suffering does not result from inequality of condition. Many a poor tiller of the fields enjoys a degree of peace and happiness that those favoured by birth or fortune would envy. Disease visits poor and rich alike; moral suffering is more especially the appanage of the so-called higher classes, and if obscurity and poverty render certain troubles specially severe, wealth and rank play the same *role* in afflictions of another kind; there is a dark side to every picture. More than this, inequality of condition is one of the fundamental factors of social equilibrium; without it, many urgent and even indispensable functions would be neglected, numerous general needs would remain unsatisfied; so-called menial work, which, in a state of society that is still imperfect and consequently selfish, is performed only in the hope of remuneration, would never be done at all; every man would have to provide for the whole of his necessities; no one could find time for self-improvement or for flinging himself entirely into those divers branches of activity which, if personal interest were absent, would make life infinitely better and progress extremely rapid. The partisans of this theory rely on diversity of tastes to fill the diversity of functions that are necessary in social life: another illusion. The inferior, painful, or difficult tasks will never find sufficient workers, whilst easy or honourable posts will always be overcrowded. To believe the contrary would be to shut one's eyes to the present imperfection of men; it would mean the belief that they were noble and lofty beings, eager for self-sacrifice, demanding only to work for the happiness of all, without a single thought of their personal preferences; it would mean seeing, in present-day humanity, that of the future in which each individual has attained to such a degree of perfection that not a single idle, ill-disposed, or stupid person is to be found amongst them, for each one would regard himself as the brother and helper of all, and the universal standard of life would be: Each for all and all for each! How ardently we desire that this were so; how eagerly we pray for that future, so far away, when we shall have grown to this nobler stature, and the present fratricidal struggle shall have given place to a lasting peace, the offspring of a higher, spiritual, universal love. Anxiously do we await it; like lost travellers, we fix our eyes on the dark horizon to catch the first faint streaks of light, harbingers of the dawn. We greet with joy and gratitude all such as believe in that blessed future and endeavour to hasten its coming, all who impersonally and in sincerity aim at the social Unity towards which the heart aspires, and especially those whose aim it is to advance in accordance with that continuous, progressive evolution based on the physical, moral, mental, and spiritual amelioration of men, for it is they who have learned the secret of Nature. Indeed, evolution shows us that, the more souls grow, the nearer they approach that perfection to which progress destines them, and happiness exists only in perfection.

To return to other aspects of the subject.

Men are born equal, we are told.

A single glance at the differences in the moral and intellectual qualities of races and individuals, at the differences between young children, even at the differences in the instincts of infants at the breast, is sufficient to prove the contrary.

There are savages in whom no trace whatever of the moral sense can be discovered. Charles Darwin in one of his works relates a fact, which Mrs. Besant has quoted, in illustration of this. An English missionary reproached a Tasmanian with having killed his wife in order to eat her. In that rudimentary intellect, the reproach aroused an idea quite different from that of a crime; the cannibal thought the missionary imagined that human flesh was of an unpleasant flavour, and so he replied: "But she was very good!"

Is it possible to attribute to the influence of surroundings alone a degree of moral poverty so profound as this?

Many a mother has been able to find out that souls are not equal, in other words, that they are of different ages, by the discovery of diametrically opposite qualities and tendencies in two children born under the same conditions; in twins, for instance.

Every schoolmaster has noticed the same fact in the pupils under his charge. Mrs. Besant says that amongst the 80,000 children who came under her inspection in the London schools she would often find side by side with gentle, affectionate little beings others who showed criminal tendencies from birth.

Looking at the question from another point of view, are we not continually finding in schools and educational establishments pupils who, for no explicable reason, show a disposition for one branch of instruction only? They shine in this, but are dunces in every other subject.

As a final example, do not infant prodigies prove that men are not born equal? Young, who discovered the undulatory theory of light, could read with wonderful rapidity at the age of two, whilst at eight he had a thorough knowledge of six languages.

Sir W. R. Hamilton began to learn Hebrew when he was three, and knew it perfectly four years later. At the age of thirteen he knew thirteen languages.

Gauss, of Brunswick—the greatest mathematician in Europe, according to Laplace—solved problems in arithmetic when only three.

No, men are not born equal. Nor does environment cause the inequalities we find; it favours or checks the development of qualities, but has no part in their creation. Still, its influence is sufficiently important for us to give it due consideration.

We are linked to one another by the closest bonds of solidarity, whether we wish it and are conscious thereof or not. Everything absorbs and throws off, breathes in and breathes out, and this universal exchange, if at times bad, is none the less a powerful factor in evolution. The atom of carbon, on entering into the combinations of the human body, is endowed with a far higher power of combining than the one which has just left the lump of ore; to obtain its new properties, this atom has had to pass through millions of vegetable, animal, and human molecules. Animals brought into close contact with man develop mentally to a degree that is sometimes incredible, by reason of the intellectual food with which our thoughts supply them. The man who lives alone is, other things being equal, weaker physically, morally, and mentally than he who lives in a large social environment; it is for this reason that the mind develops far more rapidly in large centres of life than in the country. And what is true of good is, unfortunately, true also of evil qualities.

Consequently, environment has an undeniable influence, and it is perfectly true to say that the social conditions under which individuals are born favour or impede the development of their faculties. There its influence stops; it can intensify inequality, but does not create it.

Inequality of condition arises, above all else, from the continuity of what might be called creation. Atoms are incessantly being formed in the womb of the Virgin Mother,[22] by the might of the divine vortex perceived by seers in ecstatic vision, and which theosophy has named the Great Breath; ceaselessly are these atoms entering into multitudes of organisms, ceaselessly is the plan of evolution being worked—some ending, others beginning the great

Pilgrimage. It is the existence of this circuit which creates and keeps complete the hierarchy of beings, brings into existence and perpetuates the known and the unknown kingdoms of Nature; souls ascend slowly from one kingdom to another, whilst the places they leave are filled by new-comers, by younger souls.

A second cause of human inequality is the difference in effort and deed accomplished by the will of human beings who have reached a certain point in evolution. As soon as this will is guided by intelligence and the moral sense, it hastens or delays individual evolution, makes it easy when it acts in harmony with divine Law—by doing what is called "good"—or disturbs evolution by pain, when it opposes this Law, by doing "evil." By modifying the direction of the Law, the Soul engenders beneficent or maleficent forces, which, after having played in the universe within the limit the law has imposed on them, return to their starting point—man. From that time, one understands that the balance of the scales in different individuals becomes unequal. These effects of the will influence to a noticeable degree the life during which they have originated; they are preserved in a latent condition after death, and appear again in future returns to earth.

Thus are men born laden with the results of their past and in possession of the capacities they have developed in the course of their evolution. Those whom the difficulties of life have filled with energy in the past return to existence on earth possessed of that might which the world admires; now it is perseverance or courage; now patient calm or violence, which is the stronger, according to the aspect of the energy developed. Others, again, are born feeble and devoid of energy; their former lives have been too easy. Men are philosophers or mathematicians, artists or *savants*, from the very cradle.

Objections have been brought against the doctrine of Rebirth by opponents who have looked only on one side of the individual life, and so have been unable to explain apparent anomalies, especially in those cases where it is seen that the effect does not immediately follow the cause. In reality, every force that emerges from a centre of will[23] describes an ellipse, so to speak, which travels through a net-work of other ellipses generated by thousands of other centres of energy, and is accelerated or retarded in its course, according to the direction and nature of the forces with which it is connected. It is for this reason that certain actions meet with their reward or their punishment almost immediately. Then the people say: "It is the finger of God!" In other cases, again, and these are the most numerous, the reaction is postponed; the noble-hearted man, who has made sacrifices the whole of his life, seems to receive in exchange nothing but misfortune and pain, whilst close by the wicked, selfish man prospers and thrives exceedingly. Thereupon the ignorant say: "There is no God, for there is no justice."

Not so! It is impossible to defeat Justice; though, in the interests of evolving beings, it may allow the forces around to accelerate or retard its progress. Nothing is ever lost; causes that have not fructified remain potential; and, like the grain of corn gathered thousands of years ago, grow and develop as soon as favourable soil and environment are offered them. Debts are still recorded, when the perishable sheaths of our physical bodies have been cast off; they come up for future payment, often in the next life. But this next life may not wipe off the whole of the liabilities, so the process is continued for several successive existences, and this has given rise to the saying that the sins of the parents[24] are visited upon the children[25] unto the seventh generation.[26]

Such is the truth.

Souls, equal in potentialities whilst dormant as germs in the womb of Being, become unequal, as soon as they are born into existence in the manifested Universe, for they find predecessors, elder souls in front of them; inequality is intensified when they have reached the human stage, where intelligence and will come into play, for henceforth, inequality in the actions of individuals, variations of what might be called merit and demerit, set up a second factor in the inequality of conditions. Evolution treasures up the causes that have not been able to germinate in one existence, and, by successive returns to earth, realises the aims and ends of that Justice which governs the Universe, the designs of that Love which makes for progress and leads to perfection.

OBJECTION

An apparently serious objection to the doctrine of Rebirth is constantly being made. It is unjust and useless, people say, to be punished for misdeeds that are forgotten. As this objection has reference to moral proofs, we must deal with it here.

Does forgetfulness efface faults or destroy their consequences? Could the assassin, who has lost all memory of the crime committed the previous evening, change his deed or its results in the slightest degree? Rebirths are nothing more than the morrows of former lives, and though the merciful waters of Lethe have effaced their memory, the forces stored up in the soul, during the ages, perform their work all the same in the future.

On the other hand, injustice would exist, and that under a very cruel aspect, were memory to continue; for the painful vision of a past always full of weaknesses, even when free from the stain of crime, would be a continual one. And if, too—as our opponents would prefer—man knew why he was punished, *i.e.*, if he knew that each of these past errors and faults, ever present before his eyes, would carry with it a particular fruit, and that strict payment would be exacted at every step in his new life, would not the punishment be far greater than the sin? Would there not rise from every human heart an outcry of blasphemy against a God who, by means of memory, transformed life into an endless torment, destroying all activity or initiative in the anxiety of expectancy, in a word, stifling the present beneath the heavy nightmare of the past?

Men, though so unjust and little disposed to pity, have always refused to inflict on a man condemned to death the torture of anticipation; only at the last moment is he informed of the rejection of his appeal for mercy. Could divine Law be less compassionate than human law?

Is it not rash for us, in our profound ignorance, to criticise the workings of a boundless Wisdom? He who takes only a few steps along the pathway of Knowledge, or enters, however slightly, into the secret of the works of God, obtains the proof that Providence leaves no part of the Cosmos, no being anywhere, deprived of its fatherly care and protection. When, in our blindness, we imagine injustice, a void or an imperfection of any kind, a radiant beam of light shows us the omnipresent Life, bestowing love on all its children without distinction, from the slumbering atom to the glorious planetary Spirit, whose consciousness is so vast as to enfold the Universe.

It is more especially after death that the soul, set free from its illusory sheaths, makes an impartial review of its recent incarnation, attentively following its actions and their consequences, noting its errors and failures, along with their motives and causes. In this school it grows in knowledge and power; and when, in a future incarnation, the same difficulties present themselves anew, it is better equipped for the struggle; what has been learned, is retained within the soul; it knows, where formerly it was ignorant, and by the "voice of conscience," tells the personality[27] what its duty is. This wisdom, sifted from the panorama of a thousand past images, is the best of all memories, for on those numerous occasions when a decision must be arrived at on the spur of the moment it would not be possible to summon forth from the depths of the past such groups of memories as refer to the decision to be reached, to see the events over again, and deduce therefrom a line of conduct. The lesson must have been learnt and thoroughly assimilated during the enlightened peace and calm of the Hereafter; then only is the soul ready to respond without delay, and its command is distinct; its judgment, sure; do this, avoid that.

When a soul, in the course of evolution, has succeeded in impressing its vibration—its thought—on a brain which it has refined and made responsive by a training which purifies the entire nature of the man, it is able to transmit to the incarnated consciousness the memory of its past lives; but this memory then ceases to be painful or dangerous, for the soul has not only exhausted the greater part of its karma of suffering, it also possesses the strength necessary to sustain its personality, whenever a foreboding of what we call misfortune comes upon it.

In the divine work everything comes in its own time, and we recognise the perfection of the Creator by the perfect concatenation of all creation.

Reincarnation is so intimately bound up with the Law of Causality, and receives from it such powerful support, that

Th. Pascal

this chapter would be left in a very incomplete form were we not to say a few words on Karma.

THE LAW OF CAUSALITY (Karma).[28]

Karma is the Law of the Universe, the expression of divine Will. Its seemingly essential attributes are Justice and Love; it neither punishes nor rewards, but adjusts things, restores disturbed balance and harmony, brings back evolving souls to the right path and teaches them Law.

When a man acts against the Law, he is like a swimmer, struggling against the current of a rapid river; his strength fails, and he is borne away.

So does God bear away, in spite of all their efforts, those who, whether ignorantly or consciously, fight against the Law, for it is His love that wills evolution, *i.e.*, the making human beings divine; so he brings them back to the path, in spite of themselves, every time they wander astray.

"God is patient because He is eternal," it has been said. The sentence is incomplete and must be changed, since it attributes to Divinity a vindictive nature. The Law is patient because it is perfect in Wisdom, Power, and Love.

This Law is the divine Will which moves all things and vibrates everywhere; it is the music of the spheres, the song of glory and harmony, which murmurs in the heart like the rippling of a waterfall, the chant of life and joy that eternally triumphs in its never-ending creation of beings, who, after revolving for a moment in the universe, have become perfect.

Its glorious strains resound in the heart of man, when the

soul has found peace in the Law, and we are told that, when once heard, its divine accents continue for ever, like an ineffable whisper which brings us back to hope and faith, when we are sunk in the depths of despair.

God limited himself in order to become incarnate in the Universe: He is the Soul of the world. His will is exerted everywhere, it finds its reflection in every creature; and man, a portion of divinity in course of evolution, possesses a germ of will that is infinite in its essence, and consequently capable of limitless development; God respects this will in His creatures, and submits to violence, in order to teach them His will, which is supreme Love. Like a stone that falls into a tranquil lake, a human action creates, all round, concentric ripples which continue to the very shores or limits of the Universe; then the wave is thrown back upon itself, returns to its starting-point, and the man who began the first movement receives a recoil exactly equivalent to the original impetus. Reaction is equal to action; obstacles on the way may delay its return or break up its energy, but the time comes when the fractions return to the centre that generates the disturbance, which thus receives from the Law a perfectly just retribution.

The principal element in actions is thought. Every thought is a form in a state of vibration—a ray of intelligence which unites itself with subtle matter[29] and forms a being, of which this matter is the body, and thought, the soul. This being, often called a "thought-form," possesses form, duration, and strength that bear a strict relation to the energy of the thought that created it; if it embodies a soul of hatred, it will react on the man who harbours this thought, and on all who come into contact with him, as a leaven of destruction, but if it is guided by love it will be, as it were, the incarnation of some beneficent power.

In certain cases its action is expressed visibly and rapidly; for instance, a venomous thought may[30] cause the death of the person against whom it is directed—this is one aspect of the "evil eye"—as also it may[31] return to its starting-point and kill the one who generated it, by the recoil. Every mental projection of a criminal nature, however, by no means necessarily reaches the object aimed at; a sorcerer, for instance, could no more injure one who was positive, consciously and willingly good, than he could cause a grain of corn to sprout on a block of granite; favourable soil is needed to enable the seed of evil to take root in a man's heart; otherwise, the evil recoils with its full force upon the one who sent it forth and who is an irresistible magnet, for he is its very "life-centrc."

Thoughts cling to their creator and attract towards this latter those of a similar nature floating about in the invisible world, for they instinctively come to vitalise and invigorate themselves by contact with him; they radiate around him a contagious atmosphere of good or evil, and when they have left him, hover about, at the caprice of the various currents, impelling those they touch towards the goal to which they are making. They even recoil on the visible form of their generator; it is for this reason that physical is closely connected with moral well-being, and most of our diseases are nothing else than the outer expression of the hidden leaven of passion. When the action of this latter is sudden and powerful, diseases may be the immediate consequence thereof; blinded by materialism, certain doctors seldom acknowledge their real cause; and yet instances of hair turning white in a single night are too numerous to be refuted, congestion of the brain brought on by a fit of anger, jaundice and other grave maladies caused by grief and trouble, are to be met with continually.

When the mental forces which disturb the physical organs

meet with obstacles which prevent their immediate outlet, they accumulate, like the electric fluid in a condenser, until an unexpected contact produces a discharge; this condensation often persists for a whole life in a latent condition, and is preserved intact for a future incarnation; this is the cause of original vices, which, incorporated in the etheric double, react upon the organic texture of the body. This also explains why each individual possesses an *ensemble* of pathological predispositions often radically different from those heredity should have bequeathed to him; it is also, to some extent, the key to physiognomy, for every single feature bears either the stamp of our passions or the halo of our virtues.

Thought creates lasting bonds between human beings; love and hatred enchain certain individuals to one another for a whole series of incarnations; many a victim of the past is to be found again in those unnatural sons who send a thrill of horror through society when it hears of some heinous crime—they have become the torturers of their former oppressors. In other cases, it is love which attracts and unites in renewed affection those who formerly loved one another—they return to earth as brothers, sisters, fathers, mothers, husbands or wives.

But if we are the slaves of the past, if fate compels us to reap what we have sown, we yet have the future in our hands, for we can tear up the weeds, and in their place sow useful plants. Just as, by means of physical hygiene, we can change within a few years the nature of the constituents that make up our bodies, so also, by a process of moral hygiene, we can purify our passions and then turn their strength in the direction of good. According as we will, so do we actually become, good or bad; every man who has taken his evolution in hand notices this rapid transformation of his personality, and sees his successive "egos" rise step by step, so to speak, throughout his whole life. Speaking generally, the first part of life is the expression of the distant past—of former lives—the second is a mixture of the past and of the energies of the present incarnation; the end of life is nothing but a sinking into an ever-deepening rut for those who crystallise in only one direction; the force of habit sets up its reign, and man finds himself bound by the chains he himself has forged. This is the reason an old man does not like the present times; he has stopped whilst time has advanced, and he is now being carried along like the flotsam and jetsam of a wreck; the very tastes and habits of his contemporaries violently clashing with his beloved past. Speak not to him of progress or evolution, he has brought himself into a state of complete immobility, and he will discover no favourable field of action nor will he acquire real energy until he has drunk of the waters of Lethe in a rest-giving Hereafter and a new body supplies his will with an instrument having the obedient suppleness of youth.

H. P. Blavatsky, in the *Secret Doctrine*, has well described this progressive enmeshing of man in the net he himself is weaving.

"Those who believe in Karma have to believe in destiny, which, from birth to death, every man is weaving, thread by thread, around himself, as a spider his web; and this destiny is guided either by the heavenly voice of the invisible prototype outside of us, or by our more intimate *astral* or inner man, who is but too often the evil genius of the embodied entity called man. Both these lead on the outward man, but one of them must prevail; and from the very beginning of the invisible affray the stern and implacable *Law of Compensation* steps in and takes its course, faithfully following the fluctuations of the fight. When the last strand is woven, the man is seemingly enwrapped in the net-work of his own doing, then he finds himself completely under the empire of this *self-made* destiny...."

She adds shortly afterwards:

"An Occultist or a philosopher will not speak of the goodness or cruelty of Providence; but, identifying it with Karma-Nemesis, he will teach that nevertheless it guards the good and watches over them in this as in future lives; and that it punishes the evil-doer, aye, even to his seventh rebirth, so long, in short, as the effect of his having thrown into perturbation even the smallest atom in the Infinite World of harmony, has not been finally readjusted. For the only decree of Karma—an eternal and immutable decree—is absolute Harmony in the world of matter as it is in the world of Spirit. It is not, therefore, Karma that rewards or punishes, but it is we who reward or punish ourselves, according to whether we work with, through, and along with nature, abiding by the laws on which that Harmony depends, or—break them.

"Nor would the ways of Karma be inscrutable, were men to work in union and harmony instead of disunion and strife. For our ignorance of those ways—which one portion of mankind calls the ways of Providence, dark and intricate, while another sees in them the action of blind Fatalism, and a third, simple chance, with neither gods nor devils to guide them—would surely disappear, if we would but attribute all these to their correct cause....

"We stand bewildered before the mystery of our own making, and the riddle of life that we will not solve, and then accuse the great Sphinx of devouring us. But verily, there is not an accident in our lives, not a mis-shapen day or a misfortune, that could not be traced back to our own doings in this or in another life...."

On the same subject, Mrs. Sinnett says in *The Purpose*

of Theosophy:

"Every individual is making Karma either good or bad in every action and thought of his daily round, and is at the same time working out in this life the Karma brought about by the acts and desires of the last. When we see people afflicted by congenital ailments, it may be safely assumed that these ailments are the inevitable results of causes started by the same in a previous birth. It may be argued that, as these afflictions are hereditary, they can have nothing to do with a past incarnation; but it must be remembered that the ego, the real man, the individuality, has no spiritual origin in the parentage by which it is re-embodied, but is drawn by the affinities which its previous mode of life attracted round it into the current that carries it, when the time comes for re-birth, to the home best fitted for the development of those tendencies....

"This doctrine of Karma, when properly understood, is well calculated to guide and assist those who realise its truth to a higher and better mode of life; for it must not be forgotten that not only our actions, but our thoughts also, are most assuredly followed by a crowd of circumstances that will influence for good or for evil our own future; and, what is still more important, the future of many of our fellow-creatures. If sins of omission and commission could in any case be only self-regarding, the effect on the sinner's Karma would be a matter of minor consequence. The fact that every thought and act through life carries with it, for good or evil, a corresponding influence on the members of the human family renders a strict sense of justice, morality, and unselfishness so necessary to future happiness and progress. A crime once committed, an evil thought sent out from the mind, are past recall—no amount of repentance can wipe out their results on the future....

"Repentance, if sincere, will deter a man from repeating errors; it cannot save him or others from the effects of those already produced, which will most unerringly overtake him either in this life or in the next rebirth."

We will also quote a few lines from E. D. Walker in *Reincarnation*:

"Briefly, the doctrine of Karma is that we have made ourselves what we are by former actions, and are building our future eternity by present actions. There is no destiny but what we ourselves determine. There is no salvation or condemnation except what we ourselves bring about.... Because it offers no shelter for culpable actions and necessitates a sterling manliness, it is less welcome to weak natures than the easy religious tenets of vicarious atonement, intercessions, forgiveness, and death-bed conversions....

"In the domain of eternal justice, the offence and the punishment are inseparably connected as the same event, because there is no real distinction between the action and its outcome.

"It is Karma, or our old acts, that bring us back into earthly life. The spirit's abode changes according to its Karma, and this Karma forbids any long continuance in one condition, because it is always changing. So long as action is governed by material and selfish motives, just so long must the effect of that action be manifested in physical rebirths. Only the perfectly selfless man can elude the gravitation of material life. Few have attained this, but it is the goal of mankind."

The danger of a too brief explanation of the law of Causality consists in the possibility of being imperfectly understood, and consequently of favouring the doctrine of fatalism.

"Why act at all, the objection will be urged, if everything is foreseen by the Law? Why stretch out a hand to the man who falls into the water before our very eyes? Is not the Law strong enough to save him, if he is not to die; and if he is, have we any right to interfere?...

"Such reasoning arises from ignorance and egoism."

"Yes, the law is powerful enough to prevent the man from drowning, and also to prevent the possibility of his being saved by some passer-by, who has been moved to pity by the sight; to doubt this were to doubt the power of God. In the work of evolution, however, God does more than supply man with means of developing his intelligence; in order to enrich his heart, he offers him opportunities of sacrificing himself. Again, the innumerable problems set by duty are far from being solved for us; with difficulty can we distinguish a crime from a noble action; very often we do wrong, thinking we are doing right, and it not unfrequently happens that good results from our evil deeds; this is why God sends us experiences which are to teach us our duty.

"The soul learns not only during its incarnations, but even more after leaving the body,[32] for life after death is largely spent in examining the consequences of deeds performed during life on earth.

"Whenever, then, an opportunity for action offers itself, let us follow the impulse of the heart, the cry of duty, and not the sophisms of the lower nature, the selfish "ego," the cold brain, which knows neither compassion nor devotion. Do your duty, whatever happens, says the Law, *i.e.*, do not allege, as your excuse for being selfish, that God, if He thinks it best, will help your brother in his trouble; why do you not fling yourself into the fire, with the thought that, if your hour has not yet come, God will prevent the flames from burning you? Does not the man, who commits suicide, himself push forward the hand on the dial of life, setting it at the fatal hour?

"The threads of karmic action are so wonderfully interwoven, and God, in order to hasten evolution, makes such marvellous use of human forces, both good and bad, that the first few glances cast at the *melee* of events are calculated to trouble the mind rather than reveal to it the marvels of adjustment effected by divine Wisdom, but no sooner does one succeed in unravelling some of the entanglements of the karmic forces, and catching a glimpse of the harmony resulting from their surprising co-operation, than the mind is lost in amaze. Then, one understands how the murderer is only an instrument whose passions are used by God in carrying out the karmic decree which condemned the victim long before the crime was committed; then, too, one knows that capital punishment is a legal crime of which divine Justice makes use—yes, a crime, for none but God can judge; every being has a right to live, and does live, until God condemns him.

"But man, by making himself, even ignorantly, the instrument of Karma, acts against the universal law, and is preparing for himself that future suffering which results from every attack made on the harmony of the whole."[33]

On the other hand, Destiny is not an immutable mass of forces; will can destroy what it has created, that is a question of time or energy; and when these are unable, within a given period, to bring about the total destruction of a barrier belonging to the past, none the less does this barrier lessen day by day, for the "resultant" of this system of opposing forces changes its direction every moment, and the final shock, when it cannot be avoided, is always diminished to a greater or less degree."

In the case of those who have attained to a perfect reading of the past, their knowledge of the hostile forces is complete, and the neutralisation of these forces immensely facilitated. They can seek out, in this world or in the next, those they wronged in the past, and thus repair the harm done; they can see the source of those thoughts of hatred that are sent against them, and destroy them by the intervention of love;[34] they can find out the weak points of their personal armour and strengthen them: it is this that in theosophical language is called the burning of Karma in the fire of "Wisdom."

None the less, there are two points in the law of Causality, which appear to favour the idea of fatalism, though in reality, they are merely corollaries of Karma. According to the first, every force is fatal, in the sense that, if left to itself, it is indestructible. This is not fatality, for the force can be modified by meeting with forces differing in character, and if no such encounter takes place, it finally unites with the cosmic Law, or else is broken to pieces upon it, according as it moves with evolution or against it.[35] Only in one sense, then, is it fatal; it cannot be destroyed save by an opposing force of the same momentum. For instance, in order to annihilate an obstructive force, created in the past, the soul must expend an amount of energy that is equal and opposite to that force; it meanwhile cannot devote itself to any other work, thus causing, in one sense, a useless production of energy; in other words, evolution will suffer delay,[36] but, we must repeat, that is not fatality.

Now to the second point.

Thought, by repetition, gains ever-increasing energy, and when the forces which thoughts accumulate have become as powerful as those of the will of the Ego which created them, a final addition of energy—another thought—alone is needed for the will to be overcome and the heavier scale of the balance to incline; then the thought is fatally realised in the action. But so long as dynamic equilibrium has not been reached, the will remains master, although its power is ever diminishing, in proportion as the difference in the forces becomes smaller. When equilibrium is reached, the will is neutralised; it becomes powerless, and feels that a fall is only a question of moments, and, with a fresh call of energy, the thought is fatally realised on the physical plane; the hour of freedom has gone and the fatal moment arrived. Like some solution that has reached saturation point, obedient to the last impulse, this thought crystallises into an act.

Many a criminal thus meets, in a single moment, the fatality he has created in the course of several incarnations; he no longer sees anything, his reason disappears; in a condition of mental darkness his arm is raised, and, impelled by a blind force, he strikes automatically. "What have I done?" he immediately exclaims in horror. "What demon is this that has taken possession of me?"

Then only is the crime perpetrated, without there being time for the will to be consulted, without the "voice of conscience" having been invited to speak. The whole fatality of automatism is in the deed, which has been carried through without the man suspecting or being conscious of it; his physical machine has been the blind instrument of the force of evil he has himself slowly accumulated throughout the ages. But let there be no mistake; every time a man, who is tempted, has time to think, even in fleeting fashion, of the moral value of the impulse which is driving him onward, he has power to resist; and if he yields to this impulse, the entire responsibility of this final lapse is added on to that incurred by past thoughts.

Among the victims of these actions that have become fatal

are often to be found those who are near the stage of initiation, for before being exposed to the dangers of the bewildering "Path," which bridges the abyss—the abyss which separates the worlds of unity from the illusory and transitory regions of the Universe—they are submitted to the most careful tests.

There may even be found souls that tread this path,[37] bearing within themselves[38] some old surviving residue which has not yet been finally thrown into the physical plane, and must consequently appear for the last time before falling away and disappearing for ever.[39] Mankind, incapable of seeing the man—the divine fragment gloriously blossoming forth in these beings—often halts before these dark spots in the vesture of the great soul, these *excreta* flung off from the "centre," belonging to the refuse of the vehicle, not to the soul, and in its blindness pretends to see, in its folly to judge, loftily condemning the sins of a brother more evolved than itself!

The future will bring men greater wisdom, and teach them the greatness of their error.[40]

At the conclusion of this important chapter, let us repeat that Karma—divine Will in action—is Love as well as justice, Wisdom as well as Power, and no one ought to dread it. If at times it uses us roughly and always brings us back to the strait way when folly leads us astray, it is only measuring its strength against our weakness, its delicate scales balance the load according to our strength, and when, in times of great anguish or terrible crisis, man is on the point of giving way, it suddenly lifts the weight, leaves the soul a moment's respite, and only when it has recovered breath is the burden replaced. The righteous Will of God is always upon us, filling our hearts with its might; His Love is ever about us, enabling us to grow and expand, even through the suffering he sends, for it is ourselves who have created this suffering.

FOOTNOTES:

[Footnote 10: Fortunately, this is a fact only in the imagination of those who are blinded by faith.]

[Footnote 11: Before men had sinned individually on earth.]

[Footnote 12: *De corruptione et gratia*, chap. 7, No. 19; *Cont. Jul. Pelag.*, Book 4, chap. 3, No. 16, et *De Peccat. merit. et remiss.*, Book 3, chap. 4, No. 7.]

[Footnote 13: "Omnes illae unus homo fuerunt." *De Peccat. merit. et remiss.*, Book 1, chap. 10, No. 11.

Theologians pass over St. Augustine's adoption of this theory, giving one to understand that he abandoned his error shortly before his death. (*Dictionnaire de Theol.*, by Abbe Berger; volume viii., article x., "*Traduciens.*")]

[Footnote 14: See also, on this subject, his letter to Sixtus, before the latter became Pope. Chap. vii., No. 31, and chap. vi., No. 27.]

[Footnote 15: The movements of "creation" and "absorption," which are called in Hindu symbolism the outbreathing and the inbreathing of Brahma.]

[Footnote 16: Creation.]

[Footnote 17: After violet and red there stretches quite another spectrum, invisible to the human eye; it is because violet is at the beginning of our known spectrum, that one might think it was not the neutral point thereof.]

[Footnote 18: The soul believes itself distinct from the All, because it is subjected to the illusion engendered by its body.]

[Footnote 19: Without the aid of the eyes, walking is impossible to those suffering from plantar anaesthesia.]

[Footnote 20: Pleasure, like every other form of sensation, produces the same results, though perhaps with less force.]

[Footnote 21: A magnetic effect or an emotion. All travellers who have escaped from the attacks of wild beasts mention this effect of inhibition, manifested by the absence of fear and pain at the moment of attack.]

[Footnote 22: Primordial matter which has not yet entered into any combination and is not differentiated.]

[Footnote 23: A soul.]

[Footnote 24: In these cases, the soul.]

[Footnote 25: The personalities or new bodies created by the soul, on each return to earth.]

[Footnote 26: That is to say, the seventh incarnation.]

[Footnote 27: Waking consciousness.]

[Footnote 28: See *Karma*, by A. Besant.]

[Footnote 29: Those who have studied thought know that it is capable of being incorporated in diverse states of astral and mental matter.]

[Footnote 30: If the divine law allows it.]

[Footnote 31: If the divine law has not allowed the action to take place.]

[Footnote 32: Man, after death, loses in succession his astral and mental bodies.]

[Footnote 33: *La Theosophie en quelques chapitres*, by the author, pages 31 to 34.]

[Footnote 34: "Hatred is destroyed only by love," said the Buddha. "Return good for evil," said Jesus.]

[Footnote 35: It is this that causes the universal force of opposition—*the Enemy* or *demon*—to become evil only when ignorance or the human will make use of it to oppose evolution: apart from such cases, it is only the second pillar necessary for the support of the Temple, the stepping-stone of the good.]

[Footnote 36: Perhaps this is only an apparent delay, for, on every plane, force is correlative, and knowledge is the fruit of many different kinds of energy. The only real cases in which there is delay of individual evolution are probably those in which *evil is done in return for evil*. Of course, we are speaking in relative terms and from a relative standpoint.]

[Footnote 37: When human evolution is completed, man passes the "strait gate" leading to superhuman evolution, to the spiritual life, which develops the next higher principle, *Buddhi*; this is *the Path*. Human evolution develops the mental principle, *Manas*; Super-human evolution develops the spiritual body, *Buddhi*.]

[Footnote 38: Here we are dealing with faults of a more or less venial nature.]

[Footnote 39: For ever, in this case, for the soul is above these residues, and, so to speak, has given them no vitality for ages past.]

[Footnote 40: In completion of this chapter on the Law of Causality, we refer the reader to A. Besant's book: *Karma.*]

CHAPTER III

REINCARNATION AND SCIENCE

The secret of the Universe lies in observation; it is for man to develop his senses and patiently to search into the hidden things of Nature.

All science proceeds thus, and the reason that savants have not unearthed the precious object for which they seek with such wonderful perseverance is that the physical senses, even when aided by the most delicate instruments, are able to cognise only a portion of the physical Universe—the denser portion. This is proved by the fact that when man has succeeded in directing into a channel some subtle force, he remains as ignorant of its essence as he was before chaining it down, so to speak; he has not the slightest knowledge of it. He can utilise but he cannot dominate it, for he has not discovered its source. This source is not in the physical world, but on the finer planes of being, which will remain unknown to us, so long as our senses are incapable of responding to their vibrations.

Because physical observation reveals only the bark, the outer crust of the Cosmos, man sees nothing but the surface of the world, and remains in ignorance of the heart and vital plexus that give it life; consequently, he calls the disintegration

Th. Pascal

following upon disincarnation by the senseless name of "death."

He who has lifted the veil of Isis sees divine Life everywhere, the Life that animates forms, builds them up, uses them, and finally breaks them to pieces when they have ceased to be of use; and this Life—God—thus spread about in numberless forms, by means of its many rays, develops in itself centres—souls—which gradually grow and awaken their infinite potentialities[41] in the course of these successive incarnations.

Still, though the eye of the god-man alone can penetrate this wonderful mechanism and study it in all its astonishing details, the savant whose mind is unprejudiced can judge of the concealed mechanism by examining its outer manifestations, and it is on this ground we now place ourselves with the object of setting forth another series of proofs of reincarnation.

THE EVOLUTIONARY SERIES

If we look attentively at the totality of beings we perceive a progressive series of forms expressing a parallel series of qualities and states of consciousness. The portion of this scale we are able to compass extends from the amorphous state[42]—which represents the minimum of conscious-ness—up to those organic complexities which have allowed of a terrestrial expression being given to the soul of the Saviours of the world. In this glorious hierarchy each step forms so delicate a transition between the one preceding and the one following that on the borders of the different kingdoms it becomes impossible to trace a line of demarcation between different beings; thus one does not know whether such or such a family should be classed among minerals, or vegetables or animals. It is this that science has called the evolutionary series.[43]

THE CYCLIC PROCESS OF EVOLUTION

Another fact strikes the observer: the cyclic march of evolution. After action comes reaction; after activity, rest; after winter, summer; after day, night; after inspiration—the breath of life during which universal Movement works in a molecular aggregate and there condenses in the form of vitality—expiration—the breath of death, which causes the individualised life to flow back into the ocean of cosmic energy; after the systole, which drives the blood into every part of the body, comes the diastole, which breathes back the vital liquid into the central reservoir; after the waking state comes sleep; life here and life hereafter; the leaves sprout and fall away periodically, with the rising and descending of the sap; annual plants die at the end of the season, persisting in germinal state within a bulb, a rhizome, or a root before coming again to the light; in "metamorphoses," we find that the germ (*the egg*) becomes a larva (*a worm*), and then dies as a chrysalis, to be reborn as a butterfly.

Ideas also have their successive cycles of glory and decadence; is not the present theosophical movement the renaissance of the Neoplatonic movement which brought the light to Greece and Egypt fifteen hundred years ago? In 1875 H. P. Blavatsky restored it to life, whilst its previous birth look place in the time of Ammonius Saccas, the theosophist, in the Schools of Alexandria. Those who have acquired the power to read the cosmic records[44] will easily recognise amongst the present pioneers of theosophy many a champion who in a former age struggled and fought in the same

Th. Pascal

sublime cause.

Races are born and grow up, die and are born again; pass through a state of childhood, of youth, of maturity, and of old age. They flourish in all their splendour when the vital movement which animates them is at its height; when it leaves them and passes to other portions of the globe, they gradually fall into old age; then the more developed Egos—those incarnated in these races during their maturity—come down into the advanced nations, living on the continents animated by the "life-wave," whilst the less evolved go to form the so-called degenerate races vegetating in obscure parts of the world. Look now at the adolescence of Russia, the youth of America, the old age of France, and the decrepitude of Turkey. Look backwards at the glorious Egypt of bygone ages; nothing remains but deserts of sand on which imperishable structures still testify to the greatness of her past; the race that witnessed the majesty of the Hierophants and the divine Dynasties is now inhabiting other lands.

Continents submit to the same law; history and science show how they pass through a series of immersions and emersions; after Lemuria, which bore the third race, came Atlantis, the mother of the fourth; Europe and America now hold the various branches of the fifth; and later on, when this old land of ours is again sunk beneath the waters, new lands will have emerged from the ocean depths to bear the future race, the sixth.

The very planets, too, come under this law; issuing as nebulae from the great womb of the Universe at the beginning of the evolution of a solar system they are absorbed back again when the hour of their dissolution strikes. Finally, the very Universes go forth from the breast of Brahma when he out-breathes, and return to him when he in-breathes again.

Everything, then, in appearance is born and dies. In reality, each thing springs from its germ, makes an effort—the effort of the divine Will incarnated in this germ—develops its potentialities up to a certain step in the ladder of evolution, then garners the acquired qualities and again returns to activity in continuous cycles of life until its full development is reached.

PROGRESS

The observer of Nature makes a third discovery. Every fresh cycle of life is characterised by an advance on the preceding cycle; every stage brings the end nearer. This represents progress, and it is seen everywhere; when it does not appear, it is because our limited vision cannot pierce its veil. Minerals slowly develop in the bowels of the earth, and miners well know when the ore is more or less "ripe,"[45] and that certain portions, now in a transition stage, will in a certain number of centuries have become pure gold; experiments[46] have proved that metals are liable to "fatigue" from excessive tension; and that, after a rest, they acquire greater power of resistance than before; magnets "are fed," *i.e.*, they increase their power of attraction, by exercise; cultivation improves and sometimes altogether transforms certain species of vegetables; the rapid mental development of domestic animals by contact with man is a striking instance of the heights to which progress may attain when it is aided, whilst the influence of teaching and education on the development of individuals as well as of races is even more striking.[47]

Th. Pascal

THE GOAL OF EVOLUTION

The Formation of Centres of Consciousness that become "Egos."

Through innumerable wanderings this general progress traces a clear, unwavering line. Those capable of following evolution on the planes of finer matter at once perceive, as it were, wide-spreading centres forming in the sea of divine Essence, which is projected by the Logos into the Universe. As the ages pass, these centres are sub-divided into more restricted centres, into clearer and clearer "blocks" in which consciousness, that is, the faculty of receiving vibrations from without, is gradually developed, and when this consciousness within them reaches its limit, they begin to differentiate from their surroundings, to feel the idea of the "I" spring up within them. From that time, there is added to the power of receiving vibrations consciously, that of generating them voluntarily; no longer are they passive centres, but rather beings that have become capable of receiving and giving freely, individualities recognising and affirming themselves more day by day; "I's," who henceforth regard themselves as separated from the rest of the Universe; this stage is that of the Heresy of Separateness. Regarding this heresy, however, one may well say: *Felix culpa.*

Fortunate error, indeed, for it is the condition, *sine qua non* of future divinity, of salvation. It is self-consciousness; man is born; man, the centre of evolution, set midway between the divine fragment which is beginning and that which is ending its unfoldment, at the turning point of the arc which leads the most elementary of the various kingdoms of Nature to the most divine of Hierarchies. This stage is a terrible one, because it is that which represents egoism, *i.e.* combat, the cause of every evil that afflicts the world, but it is a necessary evil, for there can be no *individual* wisdom, power, and immortality without the formation of an "I." This ego is nothing but the first shoot, or bud, of the individual soul; it is only one of its first faculties; the finest show themselves subsequently. This bud is to blossom into a sweet-smelling flower; love and compassion, devotion, and self-sacrifice will come into manifestation, and the "centre of consciousness," after passing through the primitive stages—often called the elemental kingdoms—after being sheathed in mineral, vegetable, and animal forms, after having thought, reasoned, and willed in human forms and looked upon itself as separated from its fellow-creatures, comes finally to understand that it is only a breath of the spirit, momentarily clad in a frail garment of matter, recognises its oneness with all and everything, passes into the angelic state, is born as Christ and so ends as a finished, perfected soul—a World-Saviour.

Such is the Goal of life, the wherefore of the Universes, the explanation of these startling evolutions of souls in the various worlds, the solution of the problem regarding the diversity in the development of beings, the justification of Providence before the blasphemy of the inequality of conditions.

A FEW DEDUCTIONS

The Germ.

From the facts established in the course of this comprehensive view of the Universe, we are enabled to draw important deductions.

For instance, as the basis of every "cycle of life" is found the

Th. Pascal

egg or germ, that strange microcosm which appears to contain within itself the entire organism from which it proceeds and which seems capable of manifesting it in its entirety. The first embryologic discovery we make as the result of this study—a discovery of the utmost importance—is that germs are one in essence, and are all endowed with the same possibilities and potentialities. The only difference that can be found in them is that the more evolved have acquired the power of developing, in the same cycle, a greater number of links, so to speak, in the chain of forms that proceeds from the atom to the sheath, or envelope, of the Gods-Men. Thus, the highest germ which the microscope enables us to follow—the human ovule—is first a kind of mineral represented by the nucleus (the point, unity) of its germinal cell; then it takes the vegetable form—a radicle, crowned by two cotyledons (duality); afterwards it becomes a fish (multiplicity), which is successively transformed into a batrachian, then a bird, afterwards assuming more and more complex animal forms, until, about the third month of foetal life, it appears in the human form.

The process of transformation is more rapid when Nature has repeated it a certain number of times; it then represents a more extensive portion of the ladder of evolution, but, be it noted, the process is the same for all, and for all the ladder is composed of the same number of steps; beings start from the same point, follow the same path and halt at the same stages; nothing but their age causes their inequalities. They are more than brothers, they are all representatives of the One, that which is at the root of the Universe, Divinity, supreme Being.

We also see that progress, the result of the conservation of qualities, offers us repeated instances of these stages in the reappearance, at each step of the ladder, of the forms preceding it in the natural series. In the course of its evolution, the germ of an animal passes through the mineral and vegetable forms; if the animal is a bird, its final embryological form will be preceded by the animal forms, which, in the evolutionary series, make their appearance before the avian type; if we are dealing with a mammifer, the animal will be the summit of all the lower types; when it is the human germ that we are following in its development, we see that it also has contained within itself and is successively reproducing the potentialities of the whole preceding series. The microscope is able to show only clearly marked stages and the most characteristic types, for evolution runs through its initial stages with a rapidity defying the closest physical observation. If only Nature would slacken her pace in order to humour our incapacity, we should see in an even more striking fashion that she preserves everything she has attained and develops the power of reconstruction with ever-increasing rapidity and perfection.

True, each cycle of incarnation realises only an infinitesimal fraction of the total progress made, each being advances only one step at a time along this interminable series; but then, are not these minor "cycles" in the course of which brings grow and advance towards the final Goal, the visible, material expression, the tangible and indisputable proof of the strict, the inexorable Law of Rebirths?

What the Germ contains.

Now let us examine a little more carefully this process of physical germination and attempt to discover an important secret from it; let us see whether the material germ contains the whole being, or whether, as the ancient wisdom teaches, the vehicles of the divine Spark in evolution are as numerous as the germs which respectively effect their development and preservation.

Although here, too, the doctrine of the Christian churches is inadequate, we cannot altogether pass it by in silence. We will, therefore, state it, recommending the reader to compare it with the theory of science and the teachings of theosophy.

The Churches deny evolution. They say: one single body, one single state of development for each human being. For the lower kingdoms a state of nothingness before birth and after death, whatever may have been the fate of these beings during the short life imposed upon them; for man a single body for which God creates a single soul and to which He gives a single incarnation on a single planet,[48] the Earth.

It is our ardent wish that the signs of the growing acceptance of the idea of evolution now manifesting themselves in Christian teaching may increase, and that the Church, whatever be the influence that induces her to take the step, will in the end loyally hold out her hand to Science. Instead of remaining hostile, the two will then help each other to mount the ladder of Truth; and divine Life, the light of all sciences, philosophies, and religions, will illumine the dark path they are treading, and guide their steps towards that One Truth which is both without and within them.

Scientific materialism says:

Yes, everything is born again from its germ—thus is progress made, but that is the limit of my concessions. Everything is matter; the soul has no existence. There is evolution of matter, for matter, and by matter. When a form is destroyed, its qualities, like its power of rebirth, are stored away in a latent condition, within the germs it has produced during its period of activity. Along with the disappearance of matter, everything disappears—qualities, thoughts, "ego"— and passes into a latent slate within the germ; along with the return of the form, qualities and attributes gradually reappear without any hypothetical soul whatever having any concern in the matter. So long as the form is in its germ stage, the being is nothing more than a mass of potentialities; when fully developed its faculties reappear, but they remain strictly attached to the form, and if the latter changes, the faculties echo the change, so to speak, with the utmost fidelity. Matter is the parent of intelligence, the brain manufactures thought, and the heart distills love, just as the liver secretes bile; such is the language of present-day science.

This theory accepts the idea of universal injustice in its entirety; we shall shortly prove that, notwithstanding its apparent logic, it explains only one side of evolution, and that if matter is the condition *sine qua non* of the manifestation of spirit, it is at least curious that the latter acts so powerfully upon it, and is, beyond the possibility of a doubt, its real master.[49]

Modern Theosophy, as well as the Wisdom of old, says in its turn:

Spirit is the All, the one Being, the only Being that exists.

Force-matter[50] is nothing but the product of the spirit's activity; in it we find many and divers properties—density, weight, temperature, volume, elasticity, cohesion, &c., because we judge it from our sense perceptions; but in reality, we know it so little, that the greatest thinkers have called it "a state of consciousness," *i.e.,* an impression produced by it within ourselves.[51] It is the result of the will of the supreme Spirit, which creates "differences" (forms) in unfathomable homogeneous Unity, which is incarnated in them and produces the modifications necessary for the development of its powers, in other words, for the accomplishment of their evolution. As this evolution takes place in the finite—for the Infinite can effect its "sacrifice,"

Th. Pascal

i.e. its incarnation,[52] only by limiting itself—it is progressive, proceeding from the simple to the complex. Each incarnate, divine "fragment"[53] at first develops the simpler qualities and acquires the higher ones only by degrees; these qualities can appear only by means of a vehicle of matter, just as the colour-producing properties of a ray of light only become manifest with the aid of a prism. Form plays the part of the revealer of the qualities latent in the divine germ (the soul); the more complex this form becomes, the more atomic divisions it has in a state of activity; the greater the number of senses it has awake, the greater the number of qualities it expresses.

In this process, we see at work, three main factors; *Spirit*,[54] awakening within itself *vibrations*,[55] which assume *divers appearances*.[56] These three factors are one; force-matter and form cannot exist without the all-powerful, divine Will (Spirit), for this is the supreme Being, who, by his Will, creates force matter, by his Intelligence gives it a form, and animates it with his Love.

Force-matter is the blind giant, who, in the Sankhya philosophy, carries on his shoulders the lame man who can see—a giant, for it is activity itself; and blind, because this activity is directed only by the intelligent Will of the Spirit. The latter is lame, because when it has not at its disposal an instrument of form-matter, it cannot act, it cannot appear, it is no longer manifested, having disappeared with the great periodical dissolution of things which the poetical East calls the inbreathing of Brahma.

Form—all form—creates a germ which reproduces it. The germ is an aggregate containing, in a very high state of vitalisation, all the atomic types that will enter into the tissues of the form it has to build up. These types serve as centres of attraction for the atoms which are to collect round them when, under the influence of the "vital fire,"[57] creative activity has been roused in the germ. Each atomic type now attracts from the immediate surroundings the atoms that resemble it, the process of segmentation which constitutes germination begins, and the particular tissues represented by the different atomic types are formed; in this way the fibrous, osseous, muscular, nervous, epithelial, and other tissues are reproduced.

The creative activity that builds up tissues, if left to itself, could create nothing but formless masses; it must have the help of the intelligence to organise the atoms into molecules, the molecules into tissues, and these again into organs capable of a corporate life as a single organism, supplied with centres of sensation and action. This intelligence cannot proceed from the mind bodies of the various beings, for the latter manifest their qualities only when they possess a fully-developed form—which is not the case with the germs; moreover, the lower kingdoms show nothing but instinct, and even the superior animals possess only a rudimentary form of mentality. The most skilful human anatomist knows nothing more than the eye can teach him regarding the forms he dissects, though even if he were acquainted with their whole structure, he would none the less be quite incapable of creating the simplest sense organ. The Form is the expression of cosmic intelligence, of God incarnated in the Universe, the Soul of the world, which, after creating matter, aggregates it into divers types, to which it assigns a certain duration. The type of the form varies with the stage of development of the being (*the soul*) incarnated therein, for the instrument must be adapted to the artist's capacity; the latter could not use an instrument either too imperfect or too perfect for his degree of skill. What could the rudimentary musician of a savage tribe do if seated before the complex organ of one of our cathedrals; whilst, on the other hand, what kind of harmony could a Wagner produce from a

Th. Pascal

shepherd's pipe? The Cosmic intelligence would appear to have created a single, radical form-type, which gradually develops and at each step produces an apparently new form, until its series has reached the finished type of evolution. It stops the evolutionary process of each germ at the requisite point in the scale; in the case of the most rudimentary souls it allows a single step to be taken, thus supplying an instrument that possesses the requisite simplicity; the process is continued longer for the more advanced souls, but stops just when the form has become a suitable instrument. When it does not furnish the fecundated germ with the "model" which is to serve as a ground-plan for atomic deposits, segmentation takes place in a formless mass, and in this the tissues are shown without organisation; it is then a mole, a false conception.

It is the same cosmic Intelligence that derides the period during which the form shall remain in a state of activity in the world. Until a soul has learnt the lesson that incarnation in a form must teach it, this form is necessary, and is given to it again and again until the soul has assimilated the experience that form had to supply; when it has nothing more to learn from the form, on returning to incarnation it passes into one that is more complex. The soul learns only by degrees, beginning with the letters of the alphabet of Wisdom, and gradually passing to more complex matter; thus the stages of evolution are innumerable and the transition from one to the other imperceptible; modern science states this fact, though without explaining it, when she says that "Nature makes no leaps."

The building up of forms is effected by numerous Beings, forming an uninterrupted chain that descends from the mighty Architect, God, to the humblest, tiniest, least conscious of the "builders."[58] God, the universal Spirit, directs evolution, and could accomplish every detail of it directly; but it is necessary, for their own development, that the souls, whatever stage they have reached, should work in the whole of creation, and therein play the part, whether consciously or unconsciously, that they are fitted to play. Consequently they are employed at every stage; and, in order to avoid mistakes, their activity is guided by more advanced souls, themselves the agents of higher cosmic Entities, right on up to God, the sovereign controller of the hierarchies. Consequently there are no mistakes—if, indeed, there are any real ones at all—in Nature, except those that are compatible with evolution and of which the results are necessary for the instruction of souls; but the Law is continually correcting them in order to restore the balance. Such, in general outline, is the reason for the intervention of beings in the evolutionary process.

So far as man is concerned, the highest of these Beings supply the ideal type of the form which is to give the soul, when reincarnated, the best means of expression; others take charge of these models and entrust them to entities whose sole mission is to keep them before their mental eyes and guide the thousands of "builders" who build round them the atoms which are to form the tabernacle of flesh in its minutest details; these Liliputian builders may be seen at work by the inner eye; they are as real as the workmen who construct material edifices in accordance with an architect's plans.

That everything may be faithfully reproduced in form the entity that controls the building must not lose sight of the model for a single moment. Nor does it do so, generally speaking, for one may say that this being is, as it were, the soul of the model, being one with it and conscious only of the work it has to perform. In many cases, however, it receives certain impressions before birth from the mother's thoughts: an influence capable either of forwarding or hindering its work. The ancient Greeks were well acquainted with this fact when they assisted Nature to create beautiful forms by placing in the mother's room statues of rare plastic perfection, and removing from her sight every suggestion of ugliness. More than this; certain intense emotions of the pregnant woman are capable of momentarily effacing the image of the model which the builder has to reproduce, and replacing certain of its details with images arising from the mother's imagination. If these images are sufficiently vivid, the being follows them; and if they endure for a certain length of time they are definitely incorporated in the building of the body. In this fashion, many birth marks (*naevi materni*) are produced; strawberries or other fruit, eagerly desired at times when they cannot be procured, have appeared on the child's skin; divers objects that have left a vivid impression on the imagination may have the same effect. The clearness and perfection of the impression depend on the intensity and continuance of the mental image; the part where it is to appear depends on the sense impressions of the mother coinciding with the desire which forms the image—for instance, a spot on the body touched rather sharply at the moment. This has given rise to the idea that the "longing" is impressed on that part of the body which the mother is touching during her desire. When the image is particularly strong and persistent considerable modifications of the body have been obtained; in such cases, children are born with animal-like heads, and treatises on teratology relate the case of a foetus born with the head detached from the trunk, because the mother, after witnessing an execution, had been horribly impressed by the sight of the separated heads of the victims. Malebranche, in his *Recherche de la Verite*, tells of a child that was born with broken limbs because his mother had seen the torture of the wheel. In this case, the image must have been of enormous vibratory power and of considerable persistence.[59]

A general or even a local arrest of development is almost always due to the phenomenon of mental inhibition experienced by the same being; it definitely ceases to see the plan, evolution stops, and the embryo, expelled before the time takes on the form of the evolutionary stage it had reached at that moment; if it ceases to deal with a single detail only that detail remains in *statu quo*, and is often embedded in portions of the organism quite away from the point where it would have been found had it continued to evolve; certain cysts belong to this class.

The third factor, the Spirit, the Soul—or, to be more exact, the incarnated divine ray—follows a line of evolution parallel to that of the matter which constitutes its form, its instrument; this parallelism is so complete that it has deceived observers insufficiently acquainted with the wonders of evolution. It is thus that scientific materialism has taken root. We will endeavour to set forth the mistake that has been made, and call to mind the correctness of the Vedantin symbol, which represents the soul as lame, incapable of acting without the giant, force-matter; though the latter, without the guidance of the former, could not advance along the path of evolution.

This soul is a "no-thing," which, in reality, is everything; a ray of the spiritual sun (*God*), a divine spark incarnated in the vibration (*matter*) produced by the supreme Being, it is a "centre," capable of all its Father's potentialities. These potentialities, which may be grouped together under three general heads—power, love, and wisdom—we may sum up in the one word: consciousness. It is, indeed, a "centre of consciousness" in the germinal state, that is about to blossom forth, realising all its possibilities and becoming a being fully aware of its unity with the Being from which it comes and which it will then have become.

In this development the vibrations of outer matter play the part of the steel, which, on striking flint, causes the life latent within the latter to dart forth. Each vibration which strikes the soul arouses therein a dormant faculty, and when all the vibrations of the universe have touched it, this soul will have developed as many faculties as that universe admits of, until, in the course of successive worlds, it becomes increasingly divine in the one Divine Being. In order that all the vibrations of which a universe is capable may reach the soul the latter must surround itself with all the different types of atoms that exist in the world, for every vibration is an atomic movement, and the nature of the vibration depends on the quality of the atoms in motion. Now, the first part of evolution consists in condensing round vital centres[60] (*souls*) atoms aggregated in combinations of a progressively increasing density, on to those that make up the physical plane; when the soul has thus clothed itself with the elements of all the planes, the resulting form is called a "microcosm"—a small Cosmos—for it contains, in reality, all the elements contained in the Universe. During this progressive development, the soul, which thus effects its "fall" into matter, receives from all the planes through which it passes and from all the forms in which it incarnates, varied vibrations which awake within it correspondingly responsive powers and develop a non-centred, diffused, non-individualised consciousness.

In the second phase of evolution, the forms are limited, the vibrations they receive are transmitted by specialised sensorial groups, and the soul, hitherto endowed with a diffused consciousness, begins to feel varieties of vibrations that grow ever more numerous, to be distinguished from the surrounding world, to separate itself, so to speak, from everything around; in a word, to develop self-consciousness. This separation first takes place on the physical plane; it is made easier by hard, violent contacts, and the forms, in their turn, become more complex, varied, and specialised in proportion as the soul is the more perfectly individualised. When it has developed all the self-conscious responsive powers in the physical body, it begins to develop those faculties which have as their organs of transmission the finer bodies, and as planes of vibration the invisible worlds.

In our planetary system the number of the invisible planes is seven.[61] Each of them in turn supplies the soul with a form; thus, when evolution—which in its second phase successively dematerialises matter, *i.e.*, disassociates the atoms from their combinations, beginning with the denser ones—has dissolved the physical plane, the human soul will utilise, as its normal body, a finer one which it is at present using as a link between the mental and the physical bodies. Before this dissolution is effected, however, human beings will have developed, to some extent, several finer bodies, already existing, though hitherto not completely organised.

The first of these bodies, the astral—a very inappropriate name, though here used because it is so well known—is a copy, more or less, of the physical form in its general aspect; the resemblance and clearness of the features are pronounced in proportion to the intellectual development of the person, for thought-vibration has great influence over the building up of the centres of force and of sensation in this body.[62]

The second is an even finer aggregate, composed of mental substance and assuming, during incarnation, the form of a smaller or larger ovoid—the causal body—surrounding the physical form.[63] At its centre, and plunged in the astral body during incarnation, is another kind of ovoid not so large and composed of denser substance—the mental body.[64]

Above these states of matter, at the present stage there appears no form to the consciousness of human beings,

Th. Pascal

though perfect seers can perceive, within the causal body, still higher grades of matter, which will only subsequently become centres of self-consciousness.

During incarnation, the soul, in the majority of men, is clearly conscious of itself and of its surroundings only when it is functioning through the nervous system (the brain); when it leaves the denser body, during sleep, its conscious-ness is in the astral body, and there it thinks,[65] but without being conscious of what is taking place around it. After disincarnation, it generally becomes highly conscious in its astral body, where it passes its purgatorial life; and this latter endures until the soul leaves the astral body. As soon as the latter is thrown off, consciousness centres in the mental body; this is the period of *Devachan* or Heaven. When the mental body is put off, paradise is at an end, and the soul, sheathed only in the causal body, finds itself on a very lofty plane, but here, consciousness is vague, when we are dealing with a man of average development. Instead of laying aside this garment, as so far it has done with the rest, it recommences, after the lapse of a certain time, another descent into the matter of the lower planes and a new incarnation begins.

To the centre of the causal body are drawn atoms from the inner mental plane; these represent a new mental body.[66] When this latter has been formed, there are attracted to it atoms of the astral plane, and these form a new astral body; the soul, clothed in these two sheaths, if one may so express it, is brought into conscious or unconscious relation, according to its degree of development, with the two corresponding planes, lives there generally for a short time, and is directed to a mother's womb, in which is created the visible body of flesh within the centre of its astral body.

This force of atomic attraction has its centre in the causal body, a kind of sensitive plate on which are registered all those vibrations which disturb or affect human vehicles during incarnation. This body is, in effect, the present abode of the soul, it represents the terminal point of human consciousness,[67] the real centre of man.[68] It receives all the impressions of the plane on which it finds itself, as well as those which come to it from the lower planes, and responds to them the more readily as it has now attained a fuller development. It possesses the power to attract and to repel; a microcosm, it has its outbreathing and inbreathing, as has the Macrocosm; like Brahma, it creates its bodies and destroys them, although in the vast majority of mankind it exercises this power more or less unconsciously and under the irresistible impulsion of the force of evolution—the divine Will. When it attracts, it causes to recur within itself the vibrations it has received and registered—like a phonographic roll—during the past incarnations; these vibrations reverberate in the outer world, and certain of them attract from this world[69]—in this case the mental world—the atoms capable of responding to them. When they have created the mental body, other vibrations can be transmitted through this body to the astral world and attract atoms which will form the body bearing the same name—the astral—and finally other vibrations, making use of these two bodies as a means of transmission, will affect the physical plane and attract atoms which will assist in the building up of the denser body.

Everywhere the formative power of vibration is guided by cosmic intelligence, but it is effected far more easily in the reconstruction of the higher bodies, that precedes incarnation properly so-called, than in the creation of the now physical body. Indeed, in the astral and mental bodies, nothing is produced but an atomic mass, the many elements of which will be aggregated into complete organisms only during incarnation properly so-called, whilst the construction of the visible body admits of a mass of extremely delicate and important details. It is for this reason that we have seen this work of construction entrusted to special Beings who prepare, control and watch over it unceasingly.

It is because the causal body registers every vibration the personality[70] has generated or received in the course of its series of incarnations, that the vices and virtues are preserved, as is the case with the faults or the good qualities of the physical body. The man who has created for himself a coarse astral body by feeding the passions and thoughts which specially vivify the coarser matter of this body will on returning to earth find a new astral body composed of the same elements, though then in a dormant state. He who, by the cultivation of a lofty intellect, has built up a refined mental body, will return to incarnation with a like mental body, whilst the one who, by meditation and the practice of devotion which bring into being the noblest qualities of the heart, has set vibrating the purest portions of the causal body and of the divine essence (Atma-Buddhi, as it is named in Sanskrit), with which it is filled, will return to birth endowed with those qualities which make apostles and saints, the Saviours of the world.

In other words:

Matter has more remote boundaries than science recognises; the numberless grades of atoms of which it consists, their powers of aggregation, the multiplicity and duration of the bodies they form, are not even suspected by materialism.

Materialism sees nothing but the part played by matter; it denies that intelligence plays any part, and will by no means admit—in spite of evolution and progress—that above man there exists an almost endless chain of higher and higher Beings, whilst below him are kingdoms of an increasingly restricted range of consciousness. By refusing to believe in the multiplicity of the vehicles which the human soul uses, it is unable to understand individual survival or to solve the problem of heredity. Indeed, evolution is only partially explained by the physical germ; the latter, in order to act alone and of itself in the development of the human embryo should possess a degree of intelligence considerably superior to that of man. This is the opposite of what we find, however, and we are brought face to face with the absurd fact of a cause vastly inferior to its effect. Indeed, the intelligence shown by the germ is not its own; it is that of the cosmic Mind reflected by mighty Beings, its willing servants. Besides, this germ contains only the qualities that belong to physical matter, and, as we shall show, the moral, mental, and spiritual qualities are preserved by the finer—the causal—body, which represents the real man at the present time.

THE PROBLEM OF HUMAN HEREDITY

If materialism were the whole truth, it ought to explain the whole of heredity; instead of that it clashes with almost all the problems of life. Physical substance offers for analysis none but physical phenomena: attraction, repulsion, heat, electricity, magnetism, vital movement; the anatomical constitution of the highest—the nerve—tissue, presents only the slightest differences in the animal series, if these differences are compared with the enormous distinctions in the qualities it expresses. Differences of form, visible to the microscope, are at times important, we shall be told, and those that affect the atomic activity and groupings[71] are perhaps even more important. That is true, especially in whatever concerns man.

Th. Pascal

Intelligence cannot always be explained by the complexity of the brain—though this complexity is the condition of faculty, as a rule—insects such as ants, bees, and spiders, whose brains are nothing but simple nerve ganglia, display prodigies of foresight, architectural ability and social qualities; whilst along with these dwarfs of the animal kingdom, we see giants that manifest only a rudimentary mind, in spite of their large, convoluted brains. Among the higher animals, there is not one that could imitate the beaver—which, all the same, is far from being at the head of the animal series—in building for itself a house in a river and storing provisions therein.

There is a vast gulf, in the zoological series, before and after these insects, as there is before and after the beaver; whilst an even wider gulf separates the highest specimens of the animal world from man himself.

Nor do the weight and volume of the brain afford any better explanation of the difference in intellect than does its structural complexity.

The weight relations between the brain and the body of different animals have been estimated as follows by Debierre (*La Moelle et l' Encephale*):—

Rabbit	1 of brain for 140 of body.
Cat	1 " 156 "
Fox	1 " 205 "
Dog	1 " 351 "
Horse	1 " 800 "

If matter were the only condition *sine qua non* of intelligence, we should have to admit that the rabbit was more intelligent than the cat, the fox, the dog, and even than the horse.

In the same work the following figures express the average size of the brain in different races of men.

Pariahs of India	1332 cubic centimetres.
Australians	1338 "
Polynesians	1500 "
Ancient Egyptians	1500 "
Merovingians	1537 "
Modern Parisians	1559 "

This would prove that the people who built Karnac and the Pyramids, who raised to an elevation of about 500 feet blocks of granite, one of which would require fifteen horses to drag it along a level road, who placed these enormous stones side by side without mortar or cement of any kind and with almost invisible joints, who possessed the secret of malleable glass and of painting in colours that have not faded even after the lapse of centuries ... that such a race of men were inferior to the rude, uncultured Merovingians, and scarcely the equals of the Polynesians!

Science also tells us that in a child five years of age the human brain weighs, on an average, 1250 grammes—this, too, would bear no relation whatever with the intellectual and moral development of a child of that age and that of an adult man.

Though Cuvier's brain weighed 1830 grammes, and Cromwell's 2230, that of Tiedemann, the great anatomist, when placed on the scales, weighed no more than 1254, and that of Gambetta only 1246.

The physical body of itself can give no reason for a host of psychological phenomena on which, however, a flood of light is shed if one recognises the existence of other vehicles of consciousness possessing more far-reaching vibrations, and consequently capable of expressing higher faculties. During sleep, for instance, which is characterised by the Ego having left his physical body, reason is absent, and what we call dreams are generally nothing but a tissue of nonsense, at which the dreamer feels astonishment only when returning to his body on awaking. On the other hand, as we have seen in Chapter I., when the Ego succeeds in imprinting on the brain the vibrations of the higher consciousness, it is able to regain the memory of facts long forgotten and to solve problems that could not be solved during the waking state. There are madmen who have ceased to be mad during somnambulism; persons of rudimentary intelligence have proved themselves to be profound thinkers during the mesmeric trance; when under somnambulism vision is possible to those born blind and certain people can see things that are happening a great distance away, and their reports have been proved correct; certain phenomena of double-consciousness cannot be explained without the plurality—the duality, at all events—of the vehicles of consciousness.

To return to the *role* played by the germ in the question of heredity, we repeat that the physical germ, of itself alone, explains only a portion of man; it throws light on the physical side of heredity, but leaves in as great darkness as ever the problem of intellectual and moral faculty. If it represented the whole man, one would expect to find in any individual the qualities manifested in his progenitors or parents—never any other; these qualities could not exceed the amount possessed by the parents, whereas we find criminals from birth in the most respectable families and saints born to parents who are the very scum of society. You may come across twins, *i.e.*, beings born from the same germs, under the same conditions of time and environment, one of whom is an angel and the other a demon, though their physical forms closely resemble each other.

Child prodigies are sufficiently numerous to frequently trouble the thinker with the problem of heredity. Whence came that irresistible impulse towards poetry in Ovid which showed itself from his earliest youth and in the end overcame the vigorous opposition of his parents?

Pascal in his youth met with keen opposition from his parents, who forbade him to think of mathematics and geometry. He besought his father to tell him, at all events, "what was that science of which he was forbidden to think, and what it treated of." The answer was given to him that "it is the method of making correct figures and finding out the proportions they bear to each other." With nothing more than this information and the aid of reflection, he discovered for himself the first thirty-two propositions of Euclid by means of "circles and lines" traced in secret.

Mozart, at the age of three, learnt the clavecin by watching his sister play; a year afterwards he composed admirably, at the age of seven he played the violin at first sight without having had any teacher, and proved himself a composer of genius before he reached his twelfth birthday.

Pepito Ariola, the little Spaniard, was only three years of age when, about ten years ago, he filled with astonishment the Court of Madrid by his wonderful playing on the piano.

In the lineage of these prodigies has there been found a single ancestor capable of explaining these faculties, as astonishing as they are premature? If to the absence of a cause in their progenitors is added the fact that genius is not hereditary, that Mozarts, Beethovens, and Dantes have left no children stamped from birth as prodigies of genius, we shall be forced to the conclusion that, within the limits it has taken up, materialism is unable to explain heredity.

A few more words must be said on physical heredity to explain why moral qualities in men of average development are often on a par with the same in their parents.

In reality, the physical germs only multiply the organic elements of the ovule, and as this latter contains the cell-types of all the tissues, it follows that these cell-types will possess the qualities of the tissues that exist in the parents. For instance, germs of sufferers from arterio-sclerosis will supply a vascular apparatus predisposed to arterio-sclerosis; tuberculous subjects will supply germs in which the vital vibrations and cellular solidity will be below the normal, and bring about those degenerate tendencies which characterise the tuberculous subject; those of sanguine constitution will transmit a faculty for vital assimilation and considerable corpuscular production, and so on.[72]

In this transmission there are two main factors: the male and the female germs. The former represents force, it imprints on the ovule the initial vital vibration which is to be that of each of the cells of the organism in course of construction. The function of this germ may be studied more easily in animals, because their heredity is not complicated by the individual differences due to the mental vehicle. The stallion supplies the vital qualities—the blood, *i.e.*, the vivacity, *brio*, pace; physical resistance comes from the mare. To sum up, the modalities of matter are supplied by the feminine germ.

Peculiarities of form proceed from several causes. Phrenology and physiognomy are sciences, though the studies hitherto known by these names are almost valueless because they have not been carried on with the necessary scientific precision. Doubtless Gall and Lavater possessed the gift of penetrating both mind and heart, as was also the case with Mlle. Lenormand Desbarolles and the genuine graphologists; but this gift was not the result of mathematical deduction, but rather a psychometric or prophetic faculty; for this reason neither they nor their books have produced pupils worthy of the name. The main features and lines only of the human form have a known meaning—and not always a very precise one—for every physical, passional, mental, or spiritual force possesses an organ of expression in the visible body, and the varieties of form of this organ enable one to judge of the degrees of force they express on the earth plane. On this basis, peculiarities of form mainly stand; and the intensity of certain defects or qualities is at times expressed so strongly that it completely modifies the tendencies it would seem that heredity ought to pass on. The similarity of form between parent and child is not exact, because it proceeds from the peculiarities of the individual in incarnation far more than from the collective tendencies of the embryonic cells in process of proliferation.

The being charged with building the body can, in turn, considerably modify its form, copying specially striking features found in the mother's thought; certain characteristic family traits, the Bourbon nose, for instance; those belonging to strangers in continual relationship with the mother, and those that a babe, fed and brought up away from home, takes from his nurse or from the surroundings amid which he lives; all these probably leave their impress in the same way. In this case, indeed, the "builder"—who, it must be added, ceases the work of construction only when it is on its way to completion, which happens about the age of seven—is influenced by the forms of the new surroundings, and at times copies them, more or less, and we may ask ourselves if the unexplained fact of negro children being born to a white woman—the widow of a negro—remarried to a white man is in no way connected with the reproduction of a mental image of the coloured children of a former marriage.

Another fact: observers have noticed that almost all great

Th. Pascal

men have had as their mother a woman of lofty character. This preponderance of the maternal influence will be understood if we remember that the cellular mass that composes the child's body belongs to the mother, not only because this mass originates from the proliferation of the ovule, and, consequently, is only the multiplication of the maternal substance, but also because the materials that have formed it and have been transmuted into flesh have been supplied by her; indeed, everything comes from this cellular mass, the elements drawn from the amniotic fluid and the blood, the milk, which, after birth, continues for long months to build up the child's body and the magnetic fluid, the "atoms of life," which are continually escaping from it and which the babe absorbs whilst receiving incessant attention from his mother.

This exchange of atoms is of the utmost importance, for these ultra-microscopic particles are charged with our mental and moral tendencies as well as with the physical qualities; personally, I have had many direct proofs of this, but the most striking came at a critical period of my life. One day, when nervous exhaustion, steadily increased by overwork, had reached an extreme stage, a great Being—not a Mahatma, but a Soul at a very lofty stage of evolution—sent to me by destiny at the time, poured into my shattered body a portion of his physical life. Shortly afterwards a real transformation took place, far more of a moral than of a physical nature, and for a few hours I felt myself the "copy" or counterpart of that great Soul, and the divine influence lasted twenty-four hours before it gradually died away.

I then understood, better than by any other demonstration, the influence of the physical upon the moral nature and the method of the subtle contagion often effected by mesmerism. *A man is known by the friends he keeps* is an old proverb.

If atoms of life can have so marked an influence upon a man nearly forty years of age, *i.e.*, at a period when he is in full possession of himself, how much more powerful is this influence when exercised upon the child—a delicate, sensitive body, almost entirely lacking the control of the soul? This is the reason hired nurses often transmit to the child their own physical features and countless moral tendencies which last some time after weaning; orphans, too, morally, often resemble the strangers who have brought them up. Like physical tendencies these moral propensities disappear only by degrees, according to change of environment, and especially to the degree in which the body is controlled by the reincarnated soul.[73]

The most important, however, of the moral influences at work on the being again brought into touch with earth-life is connected with the emotions, the passions and thoughts of those around. The child—and under this name must be included the embryo and the foetus—possesses bodies the subtle elements of which are in a dormant state; his mental and sense organisms are scarcely more than masses of substance that have not yet been vitalised—a sort of collection of germs of good or of evil, which will yield fruit when they awake. The passional and mental vibrations of the parents play on the matter capable of responding to them in the invisible bodies of the child; they vivify it, attract atoms of the same nature taken from the finer atmosphere around, and awake in it passional and mental centres which, but for them, might have remained latent, or, at all events, would only have developed at a later stage, when the Ego, master of its vehicles, would be in a position to struggle against the outer evil influences and not permit them to have effect save within the limits imposed by will. In this way, it is possible to bring to birth evil instincts in a child, and intensify them to a considerable extent, before a single virtue has succeeded in expressing itself on the new instrument in course of

Th. Pascal

development. This mental action is so strong that it colours vividly, if not altogether, the morality of the little ones living beneath its influence, and even older children are still so sensitive to it that whole classes are seen to reflect the moral character of the teacher who has charge of them. This influence, too, does not cease with childhood, it weighs— though far less heavily—on the man during the whole of his life; and families, nations, nay, even races, each see through the prism of their own special atmosphere. Mighty and subtle is this illusion which man, in the course of his pilgrimage towards divine Unity, must succeed in piercing and finally entirely dissipating.

Our responsibility towards children is all the more serious in that, to the deep impression which thought makes on the subtle, plastic, and defenceless mental bodies of the little ones, is added the fact that, could one prevent the development of the germs of evil in the course of one incarnation, these germs, not having fructified, would transmit nothing to the *causal body* after death, and would disappear[74] with the disintegration of the matter of which they were composed. Consequently, with regard to children especially, we should cultivate none but noble emotions and lofty thoughts, so as to create centres of pure and worthy activity within their vehicles in course of reconstruction, and to turn their early impulses in the direction of good, their first actions towards duty and their first aspirations towards the lofty and luminous heights of spirituality.

One may see from this rapid sketch how numerous and important are the influences added to and blended with those of physical heredity. This group of influences, some maleficent, some beneficent, is chosen by the Beings who control destiny and give to each Ego, on reincarnation, the body and environment it has merited, or rather that are needed, for the harmonious development of its faculties. A young soul[75] still at the mercy of the animal impulses—necessary impulses at the outset of human development—of its kamic, *i.e.*, desire, vehicle, is sent to parents who will be able to supply its body with material elements of a particular density without which these impulses could not manifest themselves. An Ego that is approaching maturity will be drawn to a family that is physically and morally pure, in which it will receive both the finer physical vehicle it needs and that lofty environment which, when it enters upon earth life, will develop the centres of expression for its nobler faculties. Those who are named in the mystic phraseology of the East, the "Lords of Karma," in their choice of the race, the family, and the environment in which the reincarnated soul is to appear, seek to give this latter the most favourable conditions for its evolution. An Ego whose artistic side needs to be developed will often be born in a family which will supply it with a nervous system accustomed to the kind of vibrations required, and an environment favourable to the early development of the physical centres of these faculties; to assist a being whose scientific, mystical, or metaphysical side needs to be developed, other environment and parentage will be chosen, and it is this relative parallelism existing between the moral qualities of the parents and those of the children which has deceived observers insufficiently instructed in the mystery of heredity, and made them believe in the influence of the physical germ alone.

It is an easy matter to supply an Ego of average development with a vehicle; an ordinary body is all that is needed. There may be extreme difficulty, however, when a new instrument has to be found for a lofty soul, and when we think that, in pressing instances when the fortune of humanity is at stake and the hour of destiny has struck, certain great Souls accept very imperfect bodies for want of better ones, we shall no longer be astonished at finding that any particular Messenger, in his compassion for the humanity he has to

Th. Pascal

enlighten and to direct to the ancient, eternal Source of Truth, has clothed himself with a body of flesh the ancestry of which was far from being adapted to the expression of his lofty faculties; courageous Souls are well able to put on the robe of pain and to submit to slander and calumny when the world's salvation can only be achieved at such a cost. We know scarcely anything of the conditions that control the return to earth of the Avataras, the "Sons of God," except that sometimes great Initiates, after purifying their bodies, voluntarily hand them over to the "gods," who come down to earth—a sublime sacrifice which, like that of the Saviours who consent to come amongst us, shows forth that supreme characteristic of divinity; the gift of oneself.

Nor is heredity always realised; many a physical characteristic is not reproduced; in families tainted with dangerous physiological defects, many children escape the evil, and the diseased tendencies of the tissues remain latent in them, although they often afflict their descendants. On the other hand, as already stated, extremely divergent mental types are often met with in the same family, and many a virtuous parent is torn with grief on seeing the vicious tendencies of his child. Here, as elsewhere, the hand of Providence, as Christianity calls it—the Intelligence that brings about evolution, the Justice that controls and the Love that animates it—the hand of God or of those who, having become divine, collaborate in the divine plan, comes to make up for the imperfection of the vehicles, and they permit only what is necessary to come to each one—only what he has deserved, as is generally said: this hand can create a physical or a psychic malady even where heredity and environment could not supply it, just as it can preserve a pure soul from the moral infection of the surroundings into which it is thrown.[76] This is the reason we find that heredity and environment either fail to fulfil their promise or else give what was not their's to give.

OBJECTION

Reincarnation is not necessary, it has been alleged; the soul's evolution is continued after death in the invisible worlds in finer bodies; consequently it is needless to return to the denser bodies of earth.

In our opinion, the trials of life, so exhausting to the will, must have given rise to this theory, for not only have those who advance it never given the slightest proof of its truth, but it is utterly opposed to the law of evolution.

In a world which prefers the flights of imagination to logical reasoning we are too accustomed to regard man as a being apart in Nature; we are only too prone to make exceptions on his behalf. The patient scientific researches of all ages have laid down this universally accepted axiom: *Nature does not proceed by leaps*. It has not so far entered anyone's mind— we think not at all events—to teach that the development of the mineral, the vegetable, and even of the animal kingdom, comes to a sudden halt on this planet, once the forms in these kingdoms are dispersed, to be completed in finer worlds; but regarding man other thoughts have prevailed, as though his intelligence and his heart had learnt all the lessons this earth is capable of teaching! From the most undeveloped of savages up to those glorious Spirits that have been the Manu, the Buddha, and the Christ, we find every step occupied on the long ladder of humanity. In the lower kingdoms all the stages exist also and are utilised, each link receiving something from its neighbours and giving them something in return, thus expressing on the visible plane that gracious unity which is divine Love: love that is instinctive and imperative in beings of a low degree of evolution; obeyed by those who, without loving it, understand its good services, and actually lived by such souls as have entered upon the path of sacrifice—souls that comprehend the Unity of beings. If this earth has been capable of teaching the Saviours of the world, why should divine Wisdom send thereon only for one short life this mass of imperfect men, to hurl them afterwards on to other worlds, like careless butterflies flitting from flower to flower?

Can the evolutionary effort be so easy and simple; is divine energy of such slight value that it can thus be squandered to no purpose; is the process of creation the sport of an infant God; is the Logos, sacrificing himself in order to give life to the Universe, a prodigal, working without rhyme or reason, sending forth His intelligence and might in aimless sport and leaving evolution at the mercy of His caprice; did not Brahma, by means of meditation, which, as the Oriental scriptures tell us, preceded creation, practise the gentlest, the most rapid, and the easiest method of guiding beings to the Goal? Is it not sheer blasphemy to attribute such folly to the Soul of the world? Does not the study of Nature, at each step, belie this insensate waste, of which no human being would be guilty? Everywhere with the minimum of force, Nature produces the maximum of effect; everywhere energy is consolidated with one end in view; and yet, amid the general order around, is the evolution of man to form a solitary, an incomprehensible exception?

No, we cannot believe it for a moment. American spiritists,[77] however—for it is they who have given out this hypothesis—are not in agreement with the school of Allan Kardec on this fundamental point, and this fact is by no means calculated to strengthen, the authority for this doctrine. Did we not know that disincarnate beings are as ignorant in the life beyond as they were on earth; that they tend to group themselves, as they did here below, with those who think as they do, whilst remaining aloof from such as profess hostile opinions; that the Hindu remains a Hindu, the

Christian a Christian, and the Mussulman a Mussulman; that sceptics are still sceptics; and atheists, atheists; we should think that spirit "communications" with their incessant contradictions were unparalleled nonsense, since the "spirits" are by no means agreed on the very things regarding which they pretend to pronounce a judgment from which there is no appeal.

Fortunately, there is a reason for these divergences. Death neither lifts the veil of Isis nor brings the soul into the presence of omniscient Light; man remains what he was, with all his former beliefs, opinions, passions, qualities, sympathies, and antipathies. True, he knows a little more than he did upon earth; no more has he doubts as to the after-life, he regains a precise memory of the whole of his life here, and the recollection of many a forgotten fact comes back to him; he understands better, for his intelligence is being served by a much finer body—but that is all. Therefore "spirits" reflect both the morality and the mentality of the nation to which they belonged on earth, and in the other life are to be found friends and enemies, believers and unbelievers, reincarnationists and non-reincarnationists.

Rebirths can be established only by personal proof, by memory; now, the soul that has entered the life beyond, after disincarnation, has not reached the end of its pilgrimage; it is learning that it must, by self-purification, pass from world to world until it attains to a state of supreme and final rest; but when this latter has been reached, it has lost its lower sheaths and the memory they gave it, and when the Law brings it back to earth, it puts on new bodies, which, having had no participation in preceding events, are ignorant of the past.

Remembrance, we shall see later on, is preserved in the cosmic Memory, but until the soul has readied a sufficient development, it cannot summon it forth, and even could it do so, it would succeed in leaving its impress on the brain only when the physical, the astral, and the mental bodies have submitted to a process of purification which harmonises[78] them and binds them closely together. Then only does man know that Reincarnation is true, and takes place on earth until this latter passes into a slate of obscuration,[79] or, at all events, until the development of the soul enables it to utilise for its evolution some environment on the planet, other than the physical one.[80]

We shall be told that we are now proving what we before denied. No, we are simply stating an exception which happens in very few cases and only then to the pioneers of the race—an exception which is nothing but an apparent one and finds its place in the progressive order which unifies all the beings in the planetary chain to which we belong.

FOOTNOTES:

[Footnote 41: Each part possesses in a potential state the properties of the whole.]

[Footnote 42: The kingdoms that are invisible to physical sight are as interesting as those we see, but we have no occasion to speak of them here. Logic compels us to acknowledge them until the time comes when human development enables them to be discovered and affords direct proof of their existence.]

[Footnote 43: We do not mean to affirm that evolutionists have not committed serious errors in their theory of development. But the law they have set prominently forth is one of the fundamental expressions of the working of God in the Universe.]

[Footnote 44: The vibratory impressions that constitute the

memory of the Universe. See in Chapter 4, the final *Objection.*]

[Footnote 45: See *L'or et la Transmutation des metaux*, by Tiffereau.]

[Footnote 46: Such as the one with the magnet which, if too great a weight is suspended to its armature, loses strength, and this it only regains by degrees when "fed" with successively stronger charges. A steel spring that has borne too great a weight loses strength, and may break if subjected anew to the same weight that "fatigued" it. Pieces of iron break after being "fatigued" by a weight they easily carried before. Professor Kennedy made very useful experiments regarding the "fatigue" of metals at the time when metallic bridges were continually breaking, thus causing great perplexity in the engineering world.]

[Footnote 47: There has been much discussion as to the causes of Evolution.

In his *Progress and Poverty*, Henry George endeavours to show that Evolution is in no way brought about by individual or collective heredity. He says that the factors of Progress are: First, the mind, which causes the advance of civilisation when not exercised solely in the "struggle for life," or in frequent conflicts between nation and nation; second, association or combination, which ensures all the benefits to be derived from division of work; third, justice, which harmonises the units of the social body, and without which civilisation decays and dies.

H. George saw only these elements in evolution; conesquently, he could neither solve the problem of progress nor explain the rise and fall of empires. Indeed, egoism and war are in no way, as he says they are, the sole causes of the fall of races: the soil cannot feed a great nation for an indefinite period even if the country is prevented by emigration from becoming over-populated; the very nature itself of the civilisation of the time prevents it from continuing for ever. Modern western races, for instance, have for centuries past been developing energy and intelligence; a limit must be fixed to that particular line of progress, under penalty of destroying equilibrium both in the individual and the race.

If, indeed, man is to learn strength and intelligence, he must also develop love, or he will fail. The Elder Brothers behind Evolution control the advance of the races in accordance with the plan of God, whose servants they are.

The real cause of evolution does not lie in environment, as H. George and his school would have it: it is in the divine Will, incarnate in the Universe. It is God who creates the world, God who fills it with life, guides it and permits its development. All the laws of Nature are the expression of the supreme Intelligence; all progress is nothing but the realisation of the possibilities of the divine Will.

The evolutionary edifice is based on solidarity, and here environment is undoubtedly an indispensable factor in development; still, it only acts as the field or soil, and soil without seed remains barren.

The mind is also a powerful lever in evolution, but it affects only one side of the matter. Association or co-operation facilitates only the growth of certain faculties whilst checking the development of others. Justice calls forth only certain individual and social forces, and leaves many of them in a state of stagnation.

In a word, H. George forgets that there is no useless force in the whole of Nature; that they all collaborate in the general task, and finally that there would be no progress, were it not for the existence of opposing forces. If, *e.g.*, egoism were non-existent, those still incapable of working without the hope of personal gain would lack a powerful incentive to action. True is the saying that evil is the stepping-stone to good.

Were the Law of Rebirths known, it would prove to be an explanation of the problems of evolution.]

[Footnote 48: A few theologians have feebly affirmed the possibility of human life on other planets than the Earth, but their voices have either been stifled or have met with no echo.

At the Congress of Fribourg, in Switzerland, August, 1897, evolution was adopted by an assembly of 700 eminent Catholics—laymen and clergy. Dr. Zahn said that *although creation is possible a priori, it is a posteriori so very improbable that it ought to be rejected; that those who believe in this creation rely upon the literal interpretation of Genesis, whilst the contemporary students of the Bible affirm that the book is allegorical, that God, in the beginning created the elements and gave them power to evolve in all the forms that characterise the organic and inorganic worlds.* One voice alone was raised in protest, but it was drowned beneath the refutations of the rest. The question, however, might be asked: How is the transition made from one kingdom to another? What is the missing link? Who is to interpret the Bible if it is an allegorical book? Is it the Church which has always imposed *the letter* of the Bible and condemned all who have attempted to set forth *its spirit*?]

[Footnote 49: In hypnosis, indeed, the thought suggested is strong enough to modify organic life and bring about hematic extravasion (stigmata), burnings, vomiting, etc.... In certain ecstatic cases, fixity of thought produces analogous effects. No one who has studied these questions can have the slightest doubt that mind dominates matter.]

[Footnote 50: We say force-matter, for there is no force without matter, they are the two poles of the same thing. Moreover, what is considered force in relation to dense matter plays the *role* of matter to subtler forces; electricity, *e.g.*, is force-matter, probably capable of serving as a vehicle for subtler force-matter, just as it plays the *role* of force in relation to its conductors. Force is born and dies with matter and *vice versa*; both alike arise from the activity of God.]

[Footnote 51: The sensations it calls forth vary with the forms. That which burns us, gives life to other beings; water, which suffocates us, enables fishes to live; whilst air suffocates creatures that live in the water, etc.]

[Footnote 52: All this must be taken figuratively. God does not incarnate Himself. He is the All. To our limited conceptions, He seems to limit Himself, in order to be the Life of a Universe.]

[Footnote 53: Here, too, we are speaking relatively; in reality, there are no fragments of the Absolute. We describe the process as it seems to us in the world of illusion.]

[Footnote 54: Being: Divinity.]

[Footnote 55: Force-matter.]

[Footnote 56: Forms.]

[Footnote 57: The movement given to the germ by the union of its positive and negative forces.]

[Footnote 58: The "builders" are inferior beings utilised by Nature in every process of germination and development. To certain readers, this will perhaps appear to be an aberration of the theosophic imagination, in which case we recommend them to supply us with a better theory and to believe in that, until the time comes when the functioning of the "inner senses" takes place in them, and enables them to perceive these beings in action.]

[Footnote 59: Teratological phenomena attributable to the imagination of the mother are so numerous that they cannot be refuted. The case mentioned here is taken from Van Helmont's *De Injectis Materialibus*. The woman in question had been present at the decapitation of thirteen soldiers, condemned to death by the Duc d'Alva. In the same work are two other instances which occurred under similar circumstances: in the first, the foetus at birth was lacking a hand; and in the second, it was the whole arm that was missing; whilst, what is perhaps even stranger than this, neither arm, nor hand, nor head were found, they had been absorbed by the body of the mother.]

[Footnote 60: To be strictly logical, one should say round the only centre, the one Being, but looked upon from the side of manifestation, evolution appears as stated.]

[Footnote 61: Hellenbach, in his book, *Magie der Zahlen*, says regarding the number seven.

"The law governing the phenomena on which our knowledge is based decrees that the vibrations of sound and light regularly increase in number, that they are grouped in seven columns, and that the vibratory elements of each column have so close a relation to one another that not only can it be expressed in figures, but it is even confirmed by practice in music and chemistry.

"The fact that this variation and periodicity are governed by the number seven cannot be disputed; it is not a matter of chance: there is a cause and we ought to discover it."

In his table of the elements grouped according to atomic weight, Mendelejef also acknowledges that the number seven controls what he calls the *Law of periodical function*. He reaches conclusions similar to those of Hellenbach.

Dr. Laycock, in his Articles on the *Periodicity of Vital Phenomena* (*Lancet*) 1842, sums up as follows:—

"It is, I think, impossible to come to any less general conclusion than this, that, in animals, changes occur every 3-1/2, 7, 14, 21 or 28 days, or at some definite period of weeks."]

[Footnote 62: See *Man and his Bodies*, by A. Besant.]

[Footnote 63: The size of the causal body varies according to its development. It has been named *causal*, because it contains within itself the causes or germs of all the other bodies, with the exception of the denser part of the physical. We say denser because the physical body is double: its etheric part belongs to the causal body, its visible part comes from the parents.]

[Footnote 64: The mental body, which is, as it were, an ephemeral flower of the causal, is born and developed in each incarnation, disintegrating after the *devachanic* (heavenly) life.]

[Footnote 65: It moves more or less freely on the astral plane, according to the development of the astral body. In men of low development, this body cannot be separated from the physical, under penalty of a nightmare which brings about a waking condition.]

[Footnote 66: The atoms interpenetrate in consequence of their differences of tenuity.]

[Footnote 67: Later on, the centre of consciousness passes from the human to the superhuman state and ascends unceasingly until it reaches the centre of the Divinity incarnate in the world.]

[Footnote 68: When this centre is fixed in one of the higher bodies, the buddhic for instance, the man has passed into the superhuman stage.]

[Footnote 69: As sand, placed on a plate in a state of vibration, assumes varying forms.]

[Footnote 70: The soul acting in the mental, the astral, and more especially—in the average man—the physical body. The Individuality is the soul acting in the causal body.]

[Footnote 71: See the diagram in the chapter on the Atom in *The Ancient Wisdom*, by A. Besant.]

[Footnote 72: We have seen that the organs formed by these tissues are the special work of a particular being controlled by lofty Intelligences.]

[Footnote 73: As the building of the body is reaching completion, the Ego (the Soul) begins to make use of the new instrument. It is at about the age of seven years that the development of the nerve centres becomes sufficiently advanced to allow of the brain receiving the vibrations of the soul; up to this point, the real man has scarcely had any influence upon the body, although the mental projection (the mental body) which he has formed can express itself to a certain extent much earlier, from the seventh month of foetal life; up to this time, the instinctive energies of the astral body alone affect the embryo.]

[Footnote 74: In Kamaloka (Purgatory). The desires, in purgatory, cannot be satisfied, because there is no physical body to express them, and this causes a state of suffering which has been compared to a burning fire. This fire burns up the passions and leaves behind only the "germs," which the causal body takes up and bequeaths to the future astral body. But for this providential burning away, the passions would exist from early childhood in the future incarnation, *i.e.*, at a time when the Ego has no hold whatever upon the new personality, and when the latter would be terribly affected by this influx of the forces of evil.]

[Footnote 75: Souls are of different ages: the savage is not so old as the civilised man, while the latter is the younger brother of those strong and wise Souls who compose the vanguard of humanity.]

[Footnote 76: It is impossible for heredity and environment to supply *all* the conditions that a soul's evolution calls for, and *nothing but these conditions*; that is the reason Providence intervenes in the interests of justice.]

[Footnote 77: It is in this great body, with which we are in sympathy, though we claim the right to dispute their theories when we regard them as erroneous, that this hypothesis is met with more especially. True, certain schools of lower occultism teach it also, but they form a minority, and are of no importance.]

[Footnote 78: Harmony is established when there is vibratory synchronism of all the states of matter of the different bodies *i.e.*, when each slate of matter in a body vibrates in unison with the analogous states of matter of all the other bodies.]

[Footnote 79: When the "life wave" has ended its cycle on this earth, it passes in succession over the other planets of our chain and leaves the earth in a state of slumber. This slumber ceases with the return of the "life wave"; it becomes death when the evolution of the chain is accomplished. See A. P. Sinnett's *Esoteric Buddhism.*]

[Footnote 80: At a certain stage on the *Path*, return to earth is no longer obligatory.]

CHAPTER IV

REINCARNATION AND THE RELIGIOUS AND PHILOSOPHIC CONSENSUS OF THE AGES

In the rapid review we are now about to make of the religion and philosophy of the past, we shall find that, under many and divers names and veils, the doctrine of Rebirths has been taught from the farthest antiquity right up to the present time. There is not a nation that has not preserved clear traces of this doctrine; not a religion that has not taught it, either openly or in secret, or, at all events, retained the germ of the teaching; and if we count only those peoples of whose national religion it forms part, *i.e.*, Hindus and Buddhists, the number of believers in Reincarnation may be summed up in round figures at 540 millions of the present population of 1400 millions throughout the world. The greatest of philosophers, both ancient and modern, have regarded palingenesis as the basis of life, but whereas in the past the pledge of initiation prevented its details from being promulgated, in our days, along with the flood of light which this cycle has brought us, the veil of secrecy has been partially lifted, and theosophy has been privileged to set forth this glorious teaching in its main outlines and its most important details.

INDIA

Northern India was the cradle of the present race—the fifth—the Eden of our humanity, our physical, moral, mental, and spiritual mother.[81] From her womb issued the emigrant hordes that peopled Europe after spreading over Egypt, Asia Minor, and Siberia; it was her code of ethics that civilised Chaldaea, Greece, Rome, and the whole of the East; our own code is full of traces of the Laws of Manu, whilst both the Old and New Testament are, in many respects, an abridged and often almost a literal copy of the sacred Books of ancient Aryavarta.

The presence of the doctrine of reincarnation in the Vedic hymns has been disputed; this proves nothing more than the present fragmentary condition of the Vedas. Nothing, indeed, could be more absurd than to find that the sacred Scriptures of India had maintained silence on a doctrine which, along with that of Karma, form the two main columns of the Hindu temple; for the Brahman as well as for the Buddhist—who is only a member of a powerful offshoot of Hinduism—these two laws rule throughout the whole Universe, from the primordial kingdoms up to the gods, including man; and the principal, nay, the only goal of human life is Moksha—salvation, in Christian terminology—liberation from the chain of rebirths.

In this land, in which, along with strict obedience to the rules of conduct set forth by its great Teachers, there existed the most complete freedom of opinion, and where the most divergent and numerous philosophic sects consequently developed, there has always been perfect unanimity regarding the doctrine of rebirth, and in that inextricable forest of metaphysical speculations two giant trees have always overtopped the rest: the tree of Karma and the tree of Reincarnation.

In spite of the intentional obscurity in which we are left as to the teachings regarding rebirth from the time of the decadence of India, it is no difficult matter, with the aid of theosophy, to discover its main points. Thus we find in them the return of the "life-atoms"[82] and animal souls[83] to existence in new physical bodies; the rebirths of the human Egos are indicated in their main phases; but here, the deliberate omission of certain points which had long to remain incomprehensible—and consequently dangerous—to the masses, makes obscure, and at times absurd, certain aspects of transmigration. I have heard a great Teacher clearly explain these points to some of the most enlightened of the Hindu members of the Theosophical Society, but I do not feel authorised to repeat these explanations, and so will leave this portion of the subject under a veil, which the reader will, with the aid of intuition, be able to lift after reflecting on the following pages.

The Sages of ancient India, then, teach three distinct phases in the return-to-birth process: Resurrection, Transmigration or Metempsychosis and Reincarnation properly so-called.

RESURRECTION

The human body is a species of polyp colony, a kind of coral island like those that emerge above the waves of the Pacific, by reason of the collective efforts of lower organisms.

The most numerous of the compounds of the human aggregate are known to physiology as microbes, bacteria, and bacilli; but amongst them our microscopes discover only comparative monsters, "those that are to the ordinary infinitesimal organisms as the elephant is to the invisible infusorium."[84]

Each cell is a complete being; its soul is a vital ray of the general life of our planet; its body consists of molecules that are attracted and then repelled, whilst the cellular soul remains immutable in the ceaseless fluctuations of its corporeal elements.

The molecules, too, are animated by a vital soul, connected with the cellular soul, which, in turn, is subordinate to a higher[85] unit of the collective life of the human body.

The most infinitesimal of these beings—often called "lives"—penetrate the body freely; they circulate in the aura[86] and in each plexus of the organism; there they are subjected to the incessant impact of the moral, menial, and spiritual forces, and become impregnated with a spirit of good or of evil, as the case may be. They enter the cells and leave them with intense rapidity, for their cycles of activity as well as of passivity are being incessantly repeated.

We are all the time emanating millions of "lives," which are at once drawn into the different kingdoms of Nature to which they carry the energies they have gathered in us; they impress on their new organisms the tendencies we have given them, and in this way become ferments of regeneration or of decay; they aid or retard, pollute or purify, and it is for this reason that it is not a matter of indifference whether one lives in town or country, with men or animals, the temperate or the intemperate, the wicked or the good. The animal gains from association with human beings, man loses from association with animals; the disciples of the great schools of initiation, at a certain stage of their discipline, are carefully isolated from any inferior contact.

It is these subtle forces that are at play in the physical accomplishment of an action.[87] "For material sins," says Manu, "one[88] passes into mineral and vegetable forms." When, at death, the outer sheath of man disintegrates, these "life atoms" are thrown back into the general surroundings of the earth, where they are subjected to the magnetic currents around; these currents either attract or repel them, and thus bring about that wise selection, which directs them to organisms in affinity with them.

The doctrine of metempsychosis[89] is true only for the atoms or emanations sent out by man after death or during the whole course of life. The hidden meaning of the passage from Manu, where we read that "he who slays a Brahman enters into the body of a dog, a bear, an ass, a camel, &c.," does not apply to the human Ego, but only to the atoms of his body, *i.e.*, to the lower triad[90] and its fluidic emanations, as H. P. Blavatsky says, and she adds:

"The Hina-yana, the lowest form of transmigration of the Buddhist, is as little comprehended as the Maha-yana, its highest form, and, because Sakya Muni—the Buddha—is shown to have once remarked to his Bhikkus—Buddhist monks—while pointing out to them a broom, that it had formerly been a novice who neglected to sweep out the Council room, hence was reborn as a broom,(!) therefore the wisest of all the world's sages stands accused of idiotic superstition. Why not try and understand the true meaning of the figurative statement before criticising? Is or is not that which is called magnetic effluvia a something, a stuff or a substance, invisible and imponderable though it be?... The mesmeric or magnetic fluid which emanates from man to man, or even from man to what is termed an inanimate object, is far greater. Indeed, it is 'life atoms' that a man in a blind passion throws off unconsciously. Let any man give way to any intense feeling such as anger, grief, &c., under or near a tree, or in direct contact with a stone, and many thousands of years after that any tolerable psychometrist will see the man and sense his feelings from one single fragment of that tree or stone that he has touched. Why then should not a broom, made of a shrub, which grew most likely in the vicinity of the building where the lazy novice lived—a shrub, perhaps, repeatedly touched by him while in a state of anger, provoked by his laziness and distaste of his duty—why should not a quantity of his life atoms have passed into the materials of the future broom, and therein have been recognised by Buddha owing to his superhuman (not supernatural) powers?"[91]

Such is the meaning of the Resurrection of the body, taught in the Christian church in a form that is repellent to reason, for it kills the spirit of the doctrine and leaves this latter like a corpse from which the life has gone.

METEMPSYCHOSIS

After the disintegration of the body, the kamic[92] elements continue for some time, us a "shade"[93] or a "phantom,"[94] in the finer and invisible atmosphere;[95] then they, in turn, become disintegrated by the various forces of this environment,[96] and are lost in the strata of matter from which they have been taken. Like the physical elements (*life-atoms*), they whirl about in their environment and there submit to the same law of attraction and repulsion as that which controls universal selection; they are drawn towards the kamic elements of men and animals, and it is here that we ought to place the list of those misdeeds, by reason of which these elements pass into bodies of animals or men of inferior development. "A drunken priest becomes a worm," says Manu, "a stealer of corn, a rat; the murderer of a

Brahman, a dog, a tiger, or a serpent"—and this means that those elements which, in man, serve as a basis for the passions, at death, pass over into the bodies of animals that possess the same passions or experience the same needs.

The transmigration of human souls into the bodies of animals is still generally accepted amongst the less intelligent Hindus; it has contributed, perhaps more than anything else, to that wonderful respect for life one meets with all over India. The thought that some ancestor or other might happen to be in the body of an animal prevents its destruction; even the sacrifice of his life offered by a man to one of his brothers in the animal world is regarded as a sublime virtue, and legend tells us of the Buddha, the Lord of Compassion, giving himself up as food for a famishing tigress, that she and her cubs might not perish of hunger.

REINCARNATION

The process of disintegration[97] which, after disincarnation, destroys the physical, astral, and mental bodies of the man leaves the Soul—or, to be more exact, the causal body, for the soul is not the causal body any more than it is any of the other human vehicles—intact. Indeed, the causal body is at present the only vehicle that resists the cyclic dissolution of the human compound; this it will be subjected to only when the divine spark which constitutes the Soul—an eternal spark in its essence, since it is a fragment of God, and immortal as an "ego," once it has attained to individualisation, the goal of evolution—has formed for itself a new and superior body with the substance of the finer planes above the mental; but ages will pass before the masses of mankind reach this point.

After thus throwing off, one after the other, all its sheaths, the Ego finds that it has ended a "life-cycle," and is preparing to put on new bodies, to return to reincarnation on earth. On Reincarnation properly so called, the Hindu scriptures are so precise and complete, so generally accepted, than it is unnecessary to quote from them in detail. A few extracts will suffice.

These we will take from the *Bhagavad Gita*, that glorious episode in the mighty civil war which shattered India, and left her defenceless against the successive invaders who were to complete her fall. This great epic poem introduces to us Arjuna, a noble prince, about to take part in the strife. The two armies, arrayed for battle, are on the point of engaging, arrows have already begun to pierce the air. In the opposing ranks Arjuna sees cherished relatives, dear friends, and revered teachers, whom destiny has placed in hostile array, thus giving to the battle all the horrors of parricide and fratricide. Overwhelmed with grief and pity, his heart moved to its inmost depths, Arjuna drops his bow on the ground and thus addresses his Teacher, the divine Krishna:

"Seeing these my kinsmen arrayed, O Krishna, eager to fight,

"My limbs fail and my mouth is parched, my body quivers and my hair stands on end.

"Gandiva (Arjuna's bow) slips from my hand, and my skin burns all over; I am not able to stand, and my mind is whirling.

"And I see adverse omens, O Keshava (hairy one). Nor do I foresee advantage by slaying kinsmen in battle.

"For I desire not victory, O Krishna, nor kingship nor pleasures; what is kingship to us, O Govinda (Thou who knowest all that is done by our senses and organs), what enjoyment or even life?

"Those for whose sake we desire kingship, enjoyments, and pleasures, they stand here in battle, abandoning life and riches."

"Teachers, fathers, sons, as well as grandfathers, mothers' brothers, fathers-in-law, grandsons, brothers-in-law, and other relatives."

"These I do not wish to kill, though (myself) slain, O Madhusudana (slayer of Madhu, a demon), even for the sake of the kingship of the three worlds (the habitations of men, gods, and semi-divine beings); how then for earth?"

... "I will not do battle."

The divine Krishna then smiled upon his well-beloved disciple, and said to him:

"Thou grievest for those that should not be grieved for, and speakest words of wisdom (words that sound wise but miss the deeper sense of wisdom). The wise grieve neither for the living nor for the dead."

"Nor at any time verily was I not, nor thou, nor these princes of men, nor verily shall we ever cease to be hereafter."

"As the Dweller in the body seeketh in the body childhood, youth, and old age, so passeth he on to another body; the well-balanced grieve not thereat...."

"These bodies of the Embodied One, who is eternal, indestructible, and boundless, are known as finite. Therefore fight, O Bharata."

"He who regardeth This (the Dweller in the body) as a slayer, and he who thinketh it is slain, both of them are ignorant. It slayeth not, nor is it slain...."

"Who knoweth It indestructible, perpetual, unborn, undiminishing; how can that man slay, O Partha, or cause to be slain?"

"As a man casting off worn-out garments, taketh new ones, so the Dweller in the body, casting off worn-out bodies, entereth into others that are new."

"Weapons cleave It not, nor fire burneth It, nor waters wet It, nor wind drieth It away...."

"Further, looking upon thine own Dharma,[98] thou shouldst not tremble, for there is nothing more welcome to a Kshattriya than righteous war."

Here are other extracts of this wonderful teaching:

"Many births have been left behind by Me and by thee, O Arjuna. I know them all, but thou knowest not thine, Parantapa."

"He who thus knoweth My divine birth and action, in its essence, is not born again, having abandoned the body, but he cometh unto Me, O Arjuna."

"Having attained to the worlds of the pure-doing, and having dwelt there for eternal years, he who fell from Yoga is reborn in a pure and blessed house.... There he obtaineth the complete yogic wisdom belonging to his former body, and then again laboureth for perfection, O joy of the Kurus!"

"But the Yogi, verily, labouring with assiduity, purified from sin, fully perfected through manifold births, he treadeth the supreme Path.... He who cometh unto Me, O Kaunteya, verily he knoweth birth no more."

The daily life of Hindu and Buddhist is so entirely based on Reincarnation and on its foundation, the law of Causality, that this faith gives them patience in the present and hope for the future; for it teaches that man, every moment he lives, is subject to the circumstances he has created, and that, though bound by the past, he is yet master of the future.

Why cannot we, in this troubled Europe of ours, accept this belief as the solution of the distressing problem of the inequality of conditions, for to the weak in rebellion against oppression it would come as a soothing balm, whilst the strong would find in it a stimulus to devoted pity such as wealth owes to poverty and happiness to misfortune? Herein lies the solution of the whole social problem.

EGYPT

If we pass from India to Egypt, the land of mystery, we again find the world-wide doctrine of palingenesis hidden beneath the same veil.

According to Egyptian teaching, the theory of the "fall of the angels" was accepted; the fallen angels were human souls[99] who had to become reincarnated till they reached a state of purification; fallen into the flesh, subjected to its vicissitudes and passions, these souls had to evolve, in successive rebirths, until they had developed all their faculties, obtained complete control over the lower nature, and won back their original purity; then this latter would no longer be the unconscious purity of youthful innocence, but the conscious purity of mature age, *i.e.*, of the soul that has known both good and evil in the course of its experiences, has overcome the serpent of matter, the tempter, and voluntarily chosen the life of virtue.

The "Judgment" of the after-life is determined by the degree of purity that has been attained; if insufficient, the soul returns to earth, there to inhabit a human, an animal, or a vegetable form, in accordance with its merits or demerits.

These lines prove that Egyptian teaching has come down to us, covered with gross dross and slag, as it were, which must be subjected to careful sifting; when this is done, we see that it also sets forth the transmigrations to which the elements of the various vehicles are subjected,[100] the physical ternary[101] rises from the dead, the animal man[102] transmigrates; and man, properly so-called,[103] reincarnates, but the details of these processes have been so confused in such fragments of Egyptian palingenesis as we possess that it is no easy matter to find the traces of this classification.

For instance. Herodotus tells us:

"The Egyptians were the first to hold the opinion that the soul of man is immortal and that when the body dies it enters into the form of an animal which is born at the moment, thence, passing on from one animal into another until it has circled through the forms of all the creatures which tenant the earth, the water, and the air, after which it enters again into a human form and is born anew. The whole period of the transmigration is (they say) three thousand years."[104]

This passage evidently refers to the resurrection of the "life atoms." H. P. Blavatsky, in the *Theosophist*, vol. 4, pages 244, 286, confirms this in the following words:

"We are taught that for 3000 years, at least, the 'mummy,' notwithstanding all the chemical preparations, goes on throwing off to the last invisible atoms, which, from the hour of death, re-entering the various vortices of being, go indeed 'through every variety of organised life forms.' But it is not the soul, the fifth,[105] least of all, the sixth[106] principle, but the life atoms of the Jiva,[107] the second principle. At the end of the three thousand years, sometimes more, sometimes less, after endless transmigrations, all these atoms are once more drawn together, and are made to form the new outer clothing or the body of the same monad (the real soul) which they had already been clothed with two or three thousands of years before. Even in the worst case, that of the annihilation of the conscious personal principle,[108] the monad, or individual soul,[109] is ever the same, as are also the atoms of the lower principles,[110] which, regenerated and renewed in this ever-flowing river of being, are magnetically drawn together owing to their affinity and are once more reincarnated together...."

Certain authors have stated that belief in Resurrection was the origin of embalming, because it was thought that after three thousand years the soul returned to the same body, that it immediately rose again, when the body had been preserved, whereas if such had not been the case, it entered wherever it could, sometimes even into the body of a lower creature. Herodotus, however, says that after the cycle of three thousand years the soul enters a new body, not the mummified one,[111] and this would lead one to imagine that there were other reasons for the process of embalming. Indeed, it became general only during the decline of Egypt; at the beginning, it was reserved for the hierophants alone, with the object of allowing their physical molecular elements to pass into the still coarse bodies of the masses and help forward ordinary souls by the powerful influence of the magnetic potency with which they were charged. It is also for this reason that the body of a Yogi, in India, is interred, whilst in the case of other men cremation is the rule.

On the other hand, among the multitude of beliefs left in Egypt by degenerate traditions, there were found some which hinted, more or less clearly, at occult truths, and which might have perpetuated or generalised this practice. It was supposed, according to Servius, that the transmigrations[112] began only when the magnetic bond between the soul and its remains had been broken by the complete disintegration of the corpse; consequently they did all in their power to preserve this latter.

This belief may readily be connected with theosophic teaching which says that the affinity existing between the visible corpse and the soul clad in its kamic (astral) body, the animal soul in Kamaloka (Purgatory), is capable, in certain cases, of detaining this soul on earth, after its disincarnation, and thus delaying, for a longer or shorter period, the disintegration of the elements of the passional body. It is these elements, not the soul, that pass over into animal bodies, and, contrary to the opinions set forth in Egyptian exotericism, it is to the interest of the soul to free itself from terrestrial attraction and from its kamic (astral) vehicle, and not to remain bound down to earth. Consequently, embalming was a mistaken action, the result of an error of doctrine, or at all events of teachings that were incomplete, imperfectly transmitted, and misunderstood.

Egypt multiplied her symbols of palingenesis. Resurrection—in the sense of re-birth in general—was symbolised by the toad which then became the goddess Hiquet. This animal was chosen because it lives in air and in water,[113] because it can remain imprisoned a very great number of years without either air or food[114] and afterwards come back to life. G. Maspero, in his *Guide du*

Visiteur au Musée de Boulac, tells us that the early Christians in Egypt had adopted this symbolism, and that the lamps in their churches were formed in the shape of a toad, and bore the inscription, "I am the Resurrection," in the Greek language. This goddess-toad may still be seen in the museum of Boulac.

The Scarabeus, or beetle,[115] symbolised the "personality," the expansion of the mental substance, projected, so to speak, by the higher mental body, at each incarnation, into the new kamic (astral) body; a certain number of them were always deposited with the mummies, and the beetle was represented standing on an ear of corn, a symbol of the attainments acquired during the past earth life. Indeed, the development of the Ego is effected by that of the personality it sends on to the earth each incarnation; it is the new mental body which controls the new astral and physical bodies of each incarnation, and which is, in very truth, the flower and the fruit of the labour of life.

Sacred Egyptology tells us that the scarabeus requires to be "osirified," united to its "living soul," or Ego, which sent it forth. I will now give the reason for this emanation.

When, after disincarnation, the purgatorial life begins, the Ego endeavours to throw off the kamic (astral) body, to pass into the higher world—the mental plane—which is its home, there to enjoy the delights of heaven. Thereupon a veritable battle begins. On the one hand, the Ego endeavours to withdraw the mental body, which, at the beginning of the incarnation, it sent into the kamic body, and to take it to itself; on the other hand, the passional body[116]—which instinctively feels its life bound to that of the mental element, which gives it its strength, vital activity, and personal characteristics—tries to keep back this centre of individual life, and generally succeeds in doing so up to a certain point.

When desire, during incarnation, has regularly gained the victory over the will, the passional body, or Kama, maintains the supremacy beyond the grave, and the Ego, in endeavouring to rescue its mental projection from the kamic bonds, yields up a more or less considerable fragment thereof, and this fragment is restored to liberty only when the passional body of the deceased has become disintegrated by the forces of the astral world. This has been called the *fire* of purgatory.

On the other hand, when the Ego, during life, has always refused the appeals of the lower nature, it easily withdraws, after death, from the net of passion, the substance it has infused therein, and passes with this substance into that part of the mental plane which is called "heaven."

Such is the struggle that Egypt committed to her annals when she inscribed upon papyrus or engraved upon stone the journeyings of the soul into the world of shades. The soul— the mental personality—which demands "osirification," and invokes the Ego, its god and projector, beseeching him to draw it to himself that it may live with him, is the lower "I." This "I" has not exhausted the "desire to live" on earth; its desire is impressed on the germs it has left in the causal body, and brings the Ego back to incarnation; this is the reason it prays and desires the resurrection[117] of its "living soul," the Ego. Denon, in his *Journeyings in Egypt*, has made known to us the Sha-En (the book of metamorphoses), written in hieratic signs and republished in Berlin, by Brugsch, in the year 1851. Explicit mention is here made of reincarnations, and it is stated that they are very numerous.

The third part of the *Book of the Dead* sets forth a detailed account of the resurrection of an Osiris; the identification of the departed one with Osiris, God of Light, and his sharing in the life, deeds, and power of the God; in a word, it is the final reintegration of the human soul with God.

The loftiest and most suggestive of Egyptian palingenetic symbols is unquestionably that of the egg. The deceased is "resplendent in the egg in the land of mysteries." In Kircher's *Oedipus Egyptiacus*[118] we have an egg—the Ego freed from its vehicles—floating over the mummy; this is the symbol of hope and the promise of a new birth to the soul, after gestation in the egg of immortality.[119]

The "winged globe," so widely known in Egypt, is egg-shaped, and has the same meaning; its wings indicate its divine nature and prevent it from being confused with the physical germ. "Easter eggs" which are offered in spring, at the rebirth of Nature, commemorate this ancient symbol of eternal Life in its successive phases of disincarnation and rebirth.

CHALDAEA

It is said that the Magi taught the immortality of the soul and its reincarnations, but that they considerably limited the number of these latter, in the belief that purification was effected after a restricted number of existences on the soul returning to its heavenly abode.

Unfortunately we know nothing definite on this special point in Chaldaean teaching, for some of the most important sources of information were destroyed when the library of Persepolis was burnt by the Macedonian vandal, Alexander the Great, whilst Eusebius—whom Bunsen criticises so harshly[120]—made such great alterations in the manuscripts of Berosus, that we have nothing to proceed upon beyond a few disfigured fragments.[121] And yet

Chaldaeism comprises a great mass of teachings; he whom we know as "the divine Zoroaster" had been preceded by twelve others, and esoteric doctrine was as well known in Chaldaea as in Egypt.

The descendants of the Chaldaeans—Fire-worshippers, Mazdeans, Magi, Parsees—according to the names they received at different periods—have preserved the main points of palingenetic instruction up to the present, and, from time to time, have set them forth in the most charming style of Oriental poetry. Book 4 of the great Persian poem, *Masnavi i Ma'navi*, deals with evolution and its corollary, reincarnation, stating that there is one way of remembering past existences, and that is by attaining to spiritual illumination, which is the crown of human evolution and brings the soul to the threshold of divinity.

"If your purified soul succeeds in escaping from the sea of ignorance, it will see, with eyes now opened, 'the beginning' and 'the end.' Man first appeared in the order of inorganic things; next, he passed therefrom into that of plants, for years he lived as one of the plants, remembering naught of his inorganic state, so different from this, and when he passed from the vegetable to the animal state he had no remembrance of his state as a plant.... Again the great Creator, as you know, drew man out of the animal into the human state. Thus man passed from one order of nature to another, till he became wise and intelligent and strong as he is now. Of his first soul he has now no remembrance, and he will be again changed from his present soul. In order to escape from his present soul, full of lusts, he must rise to a thousand higher degrees of intelligence.

"Though man fell asleep and forgot his previous states, yet God will not leave him in this self-forgetfulness; and then he will laugh at his own former state, saying: 'What mattered my experiences when asleep, when I had forgotten the real state of things, and knew not that the grief and ills I experienced were the effect of sleep and illusion and fancy?'"

These lines are concise, but they sum up the whole of evolution, and render it unnecessary to quote at greater length from Chaldaean tradition on this point. Still, those who desire other passages relating to the same doctrine may find them in the "Desatir."[122]

THE CELTS

Sacerdotal India—and perhaps also Atlantis—in early times sent pioneers into the West to spread religious teachings amongst their energetic inhabitants; those who settled in Gaul and the British Isles were the Druids. "I am a serpent, a druid," they said. This sentence proves that they were priests, and also the Atlantaean or Indian origin of their doctrines; for the serpent was the symbol of initiation in the sacred mysteries of India, as also on the continent of Atlantis.

We know little of their teaching, which was entirely oral, though it covered so much ground that, according to Caesar, not less than thirty years of study were needed to become a druid. The Roman conquest dispersed them by degrees; then it was that their disciples, the bards, committed to writing more or less imperfect and mutilated fragments of the teachings of their masters. Their "triads"[123] are undoubtedly akin to Hindu teachings; Evolution results from the manifestation of the Absolute, it culminates in man, who possesses a maximum of individualisation, and terminates in the personal, conscious union of the beings thus created with the ineffable All.

The Absolute is "Ceugant"; manifestation, or the Universe, is "Abred"; the divine state of freed souls is in "Gwynvyd"; these are in the three circles.[124]

In "Ceugant" there is only the Unknowable, the rootless Root. Souls are born and develop in "Abred," passing into the different kingdoms; "Amwn" is the state through which beings pass only once, which means that the "I," when once gained, continues for ever. "Gwynvyd" is the world of perfect and liberated souls, eternal Heaven, great Nirvana.

During this long pilgrimage, the Monad—the divine fragment in a state of incarnation—undergoes an endless number of rebirths, in myriads of bodies.

"I have been a viper in the lake," said Taliesin, the bard[125]; "a spotted adder on the mountain, a star, a priest. This was long, long ago; since then, I have slept in a hundred worlds, revolved in a hundred circles."

It was their faith in rebirth that gave the Gauls their indomitable courage and extraordinary contempt of death:

"One of their principal teachings," said Caesar,[126] "is that the soul does not die, but passes at death into another body— and this they regard as very favourable for the encourage- ment of valour and for inculcating scorn of death."

Up to a few years ago, belief in the return of the soul to earth was still prevalent in those parts of Brittany in which civilisation had not yet exercised its sceptical, materialising influence; there even existed druids—probably degenerate ones—in Great Britain and France; in the Saone-et-Loire district, they seem to have been called the "Adepts of the White Religion"[127]; both in them and in their ancestors, belief in rebirth remained unshakable.

ANCIENT GREECE (*Magna Graecia*)

In Greece, the doctrine of Rebirths is met with in the Orphic tradition, continued by Pythagoras and Plato. Up to the present time, this tradition has probably found its best interpreter in Mr. G. R.

S. Mead, an eminent theosophist and a scholar of the first rank. We recommend our readers to study his *Orpheus*, if they desire a detailed account of this tradition.

Its origins are lost in antiquity, only a few obscure shreds remaining; Pherecydes, however,[128] when speaking of the immortality of the soul, refers to the doctrine of Rebirths; it is also presented very clearly by both Pythagoras and Plato.

According to the Pythagorean teaching, the human soul emanates from the Soul of the World, thus affirming, at the outset, the divine nature of the former. It teaches subsequently that this soul assumes successive bodies until it has fully evolved and completed the "Cycle of Necessity."[129]

Pythagoras, according to Diogenes of Laertius,[130] was the first in Greece to teach the doctrine of the return of souls to earth. He gave his disciples various details of his past lives; he appears to have been the initiate Oethalides, in the times of the Argonauts; then, almost immediately afterwards, Euphorbus, who was slain by Menelaus at the siege of Troy; again he was Hermotimus of Clazomenae, who, in the temple of Juno at Argos,[131] recognised the shield he was carrying when his body was slain as Euphorbus, and which Menelaus had given as an offering to the goddess[132]; at a later date he was Pyrrhus, a fisherman of Delos, and, finally, Pythagoras.

In all likelihood this genealogy is not correct in every detail, it comes to us from the disciples of the sage of Samos, who were not very trustworthy in their reports.

Empedocles, one of the early disciples of Pythagoras, said that he inhabited a female body in his preceding existence. Saint Clement of Alexandria quotes a few lines of his, in which we find the philosopher of Agrigentum teaching the general evolution of forms.

"I, too, have been a boy, a maiden, a star, a bird, a mute fish in the depths of the sea."

Iarchas, the Brahman chieftain, said to the great Apollonius:

"In bygone ages thou wert Ganga, the famous monarch, and, at a later date, captain of an Egyptian vessel."[133]

The Emperor Julian said that he had been Alexander the Great.[134] Proclus affirmed that he had been Nichomachus the Pythagorean.[135]

The works of Plato are full of the idea of rebirth, and if the scattered fragments of the teaching are gathered together and illumined with the torch of theosophy, a very satisfactory *ensemble* will be the result.

Souls are older than bodies, he says in *Phaedo*; they are ever being born again from *Hades* and returning to life on earth; each man has his daimon,[136] who follows him throughout his existences, and at death takes him to the lower world[137] for Judgment.[138] Many souls enter Acheron,[139] and, after a longer or shorter period, return to earth to be incarnated in new bodies. Unpardonable sins fling the soul into Tartarus.[140]

"Know that if you become worse you will go to the worse souls, or if better to the better, and in every succession of life and death you will do and suffer what like may fitly suffer at the hands of like...."[141]

According to Plato, the period between two incarnations is about a thousand years.[142] Man has reminiscences of his past lives that are more or less distinct; they are manifested rather by an intuitive impression than by a definite memory, but they form part of the individual,[143] and at times influence him strongly. "Innate ideas" are only one aspect of memory, often it is impossible to explain them by heredity, education, or environment; they are attainments of the past, the store which the soul takes with it through its incarnations, which it adds to during each sojourn in heaven.

There can be no doubt that Plato would appear to have taught metempsychosis, *i.e.*, the possibility of a human soul passing into the body of an animal:

"Men who have followed after gluttony and wantonness and drunkenness, and have had no thought of avoiding them, would pass into asses and animals of that sort. And those who have chosen the portion of injustice and tyranny and violence will pass into wolves or hawks or kites, and there is no difficulty in assigning to all of them places according to their several natures and propensities."[144]

Under the heading of *Neoplatonism*, we shall show that, beneath these coarse symbols, Plato concealed truths which it was then necessary to keep profoundly secret; which, even nowadays, it is not permitted to reveal to all.

OLD TESTAMENT

H. P. Blavatsky tells us that the *Old Testament* is not a homogeneous composition; that *Genesis* alone is of immense antiquity; that it is prior to the time when the Libra of the Zodiac was invented by the Greeks, for it has been noticed that the chapters containing the genealogies have been touched up so as to adapt them to the new zodiac, and this is the reason that the rabbis who compiled them twice repeated the names of Enoch and Lamech in the Cain list. The other parts seem to be of a comparatively recent date and to have been completed about 150 B.C.

The first part of the *Book of God*—as the Scriptures were then called—was written by Hilkiah, jointly with the prophetess Huldah; this disappeared at a later date, and Ezra had to begin a new one which was finished by Judas Maccabaeus. This was recopied some time after, with the object of changing the pointed letters into square ones, and in this way was quite disfigured. The Masoretes ended by mutilating it completely. The result is that the text we now possess is one not more than nine hundred years old, bristling with premeditated omissions, interpolations, and perverted interpretations.[145]

By the side of this initial difficulty we find another, quite as important. Almost every page of the *Old Testament* contains veiled meanings and allegories, as is frankly confessed by the rabbis themselves.

"We ought not to take literally that which is written in the story of the Creation, nor entertain the same ideas of it as are held by the vulgar. If it were otherwise, our ancient sages would not have taken so much pains to conceal the sense, and to keep before the eyes of the uninstructed the veil of allegory which conceals the truth it contains...."[146]

Does not Saint Paul, speaking of the hidden meaning of the Bible, say that Agar is Mount Sinai?[147] Origen and Saint Augustine are of the opinion that the *Old Testament* must be regarded as symbolical, as otherwise it would be immoral; the Jewish law forbade anyone to read it who had not attained the age of thirty years; Fenelon would have liked it to be thrust away in the recesses of the most secret libraries; the Cardinal de Noailles says that Origen, so full of zeal on behalf of the Holy Scriptures, would not allow anyone to read the *Old Testament*, unless he were firmly anchored in the practice of a virtuous life; he affirms too that Saint Basilius, in a letter to Chilon, the monk, stated that the reading of it often had a harmful influence; for the same reasons, the *Index expurgatorius* forbids the publication of the Bible in the vulgar tongue, and orders that no one be allowed to read it without the written permission of his confessor.[148]

A third difficulty arises from the fact that the Old Testament—its dead "letter" and its commandments, at all events—is no longer suitable to our own race. It was intended for a nation that was composed of young souls, at a low stage of evolution, for whom nothing more than the rudiments of instruction were necessary, and on whom stern rules of morality, suitable for advanced souls, ought not to be imposed. This is why divorce,[149] polygamy,[150] slavery,[151] retaliation, *lex talionis*,[152] the blood of sacrifice[153] are instituted; it is the reason God is represented as a being to be dreaded, punishing those who do not obey him, wicked, jealous, bloodthirsty.[154] Bossuet understood all this when he said that the primitive Hebrew race was not sufficiently advanced to have the immortality of the soul taught to it. This, too, is the only explanation we can find for the sensual materialism of *Ecclesiastes*.[155]

Consequently one need not be astonished to find that the Old Testament nowhere deals—directly, at all events—with the doctrine of Rebirth.

All the same, here and there we come across a few passages that point in this direction. For instance, we read in *Genesis*, chapter 25, regarding the birth of Jacob and Esau:

"And the children (of Rebecca) struggled together within her."

"And the Lord said unto her: Two nations are in thy womb, and two manner of people shall be separated from thy bowels, and the one people shall be stronger than the other people; and the elder shall serve the younger."

"And when her days to be delivered were fulfilled, behold there were twins in her womb."

This passage has been the occasion of lengthy commentaries on the part of certain Fathers of the Church—more especially of Origen. Indeed, either we must acknowledge divine injustice, creating, without any cause, two hostile brothers, one of whom must submit to the rule of the other, and who begin to strive together even before birth, or we must hark back to the pre-existence of the human soul and to a past Karma which had created inequality in condition.

David begins the ninetieth *Psalm* with a verse which only a belief in reincarnation can explain:

"Lord, thou hast been our dwelling-place in all generations...."

The dwelling-place of the soul, at death, is in heaven, whence it returns to earth when the hour of rebirth has struck; thus, in all generations, that is, from life to life, "the Lord is our dwelling-place."

In Chapter 8 of the *Book of Wisdom*, Solomon says in more explicit language:

"For I was a witty child, and had a good spirit, yea, rather, being good, I came into a body undefiled."

This clearly points to the pre-existence of the soul and the close relation that exists between the conditions of its rebirth and the merits or demerits of its past.

Verse 5 of the first chapter of *Jeremiah* is similar to verse 23 of the twenty-fifth chapter of *Genesis*:

"Before I formed thee in the belly I knew thee, and before thou camest forth out of the womb I sanctified thee, and I ordained thee a prophet unto the nations...."

It is the deeds done in the past lives of Jeremiah that accompany him on his return to earth; God could not, in an arbitrary fashion, have conferred on him the gift of prophecy had he not acquired it by his efforts in a past life; unless, here too, we altogether abandon reason and go back to a capricious or unjust—consequently altogether impossible—God.

THE KABALA

Contact with the Babylonians, during the Captivity, brought about a rapid development in the Hebrews, who were at that time far more advanced souls than those that animated the bodies of their fathers,[156] and taught them many important details of religious instruction. It was then that they learned the doctrine of rebirth and that the Kabala came into being.[157]

In it the cycle of rebirths is called Gil'gool'em[158] or the "revolving of the Incorporeal" in search of the "promised land." This promised land, the Christian Paradise, or Buddhist Nirvana, was symbolised by Palestine; the soul in its pilgrimage was brought to this abode of bliss,[159] and, according to the allegory, "the bodies of Hebrews buried in a foreign land contained an animistic principle which only found rest when, by the 'revolving of the Incorporeal,' the immortal fragment had returned to the promised land."[160]

There are other aspects from which this "revolution of souls" may be regarded. Certain Kabalists speak of it as a kind of purgatory in which, by means of this "revolving," the purging of the soul is brought about before it enters paradise.

In this connection, H. P. Blavatsky states that in the language of the Initiates the words "soul" (*ame*) and "atom" were synonyms, and were frequently used for each other. She says that the "revolution of souls" was in reality only the revolving of the atoms of the bodies which are continually transmigrating from one body to another throughout the various kingdoms of nature. From this point of view, it would seem that "Gil'gool'em" is more especially the cycle of atomic transmigration: *Resurrection*.

The doctrine of the reincarnation of the human soul, however, is clearly set forth in the *Zohar*:

"All souls are subjected to the tests of transmigration; men know not the designs of the Most High with regard to them; they know not how they are being at all times judged, both before coming into this world and when they leave it; they have no knowledge of the mysterious transformations and sufferings they must undergo, or how numerous are the spirits who coming; into this world never return to the palace of their divine King; they are ignorant of the revolutions to which they are subjected, revolutions similar to those of a stone when it is being hurled from a sling. And now the time has come when the veil shall be removed from all these mysteries.... Souls must in the end be plunged back into the substance from which they came. But before this happens, they must have developed all the perfections the germs of which are implanted within them; if these conditions are not realised in one existence, they must be born again until they reach the stage that makes possible their absorption in God."[161]

According to the Kabala, incarnations take place at long intervals; souls completely forget their past, and, far from being a punishment, rebirth is a blessing which enables men to develop and to attain to their final goal.

The Essenes taught reincarnation and the immortality of the soul. Ernst von Bunsen,[162] speaking of this sect, says:

"Another marked peculiarity of the doctrine of the Essenes was the doctrine concerning the pre-existence of souls. They exist originally in the purest ether, which is their celestial home. By a natural attraction they are drawn towards the earth and are enclosed in human bodies, as in a prison. The death of the body causes the return of the soul to its heavenly abode. The Essenes can, therefore, not have believed in the resurrection of the body, but of the soul only, or, as Paul says, of the 'spiritual body.' This is positively asserted by Josephus."[163]

ROME

Although Rome, above all else, was a warlike republic, and religion principally a State cult, that allowed but slight opportunity for the outer expression of spirituality, none the less did it inherit the beliefs of Egypt, Greece, and Persia; the Bacchic mysteries, previous to their degradation, were a copy of the Orphic and Eleusinian mysteries. In the reign of Pompey, Mithraism, a cult borrowed from Persia, was spread throughout the empire. Consequently, we need not be surprised at finding the doctrine of Rebirth mentioned by the great Latin writers.

We will quote only from Virgil and Ovid.

In the speech addressed by Anchises to AEneas, his son, the Trojan prince deals with the life beyond death, the tortures endured by souls in expiation of their misdeeds, their purification, their passing into Tartarus,[164] into the Elysian Fields,[165] then their return to earth after having drunk of the river of forgetfulness. In Book VI. of the *AEneid*, we find AEneas visiting the lower regions:

"After having for a thousand years turned the wheel (of existence), these souls come forth in a mighty troop to the Lethean stream to which God calls them that they may lose the memory of the past, see the higher regions,[166] and begin to wish to return into bodies."

Ovid, in his *Metamorphoses* also deals with the teaching of Pythagoras, his master, on the subject of palingenesis:

"Then Death, so-called, is but old matter drest
In some new figure, and a varied vest;
Thus all things are but alter'd, nothing dies,

And here and there th' embodied spirit flies,
By time, or force, or sickness dispossest,
And lodges, when it lights, in man or beast.
Th' immortal soul flies out in empty space
To seek her fortune in some other place."

NEW TESTAMENT

The *New Testament* is far more explicit than the *Old*, even though we find the teachings of reincarnation indicated in only a vague, indirect fashion. All the same, it must not be forgotten that the canonical Gospels have suffered numerous suppressions and interpolations. On the other hand, there can be no doubt that the early Fathers of the Church made use of gospels that are now either lost or have become apocryphal.[167] It has been proved that neither Jesus nor his disciples wrote a single word, and that no version of the Gospels appeared earlier than the second century.[168] It was at that time that religious quarrels gave birth to hundreds of gospels, the writers of which signed them with the name of an apostle or even with that of Jesus, after forging them in more or less intelligent fashion.

Celsus, Jortin, Gibbons, and others have shown that Christianity is directly descended from Paganism; it was by combining the doctrines of Egypt, Persia, and Greece with the teachings of Jesus that the Christian doctrine was built up. Celsus silenced all the Christian doctors of his time by supplying evidence of this plagiarism; Origen, the most learned doctor of the age, was his opponent, but he was no more fortunate than the rest, and Celsus came off victorious. Thereupon recourse was had to the methods usual in those days; his books were burnt.

And yet it is evident that the author of the *Revelation* was a Kabalist; and the writer of the *Gospel of Saint John* a Gnostic or a Neoplatonist. The *Gospel of Nicodemus* is scarcely more than a copy of the *Descent of Hercules into the Infernal Regions*; the *Epistle to the Corinthians* is a distinct reminiscence of the initiatory Mysteries of Eleusis; and the Roman Ritual, according to H. P. Blavatsky, is the reproduction of the Kabalistic Ritual.

One gospel only was authentic, the secret or Hebrew *Gospel of Matthew*, which was used by the Nazareans, and at a later date by Saint Justin and the Ebionites. It contained the esoterism of the One-Religion, and Saint Jerome, who found this gospel in the library of Caesarea about the end of the fourth century, says that he "received permission to translate it from the Nazareans of Beroea."

These considerations prove that interested and narrow-minded writers selected from the mass of existing traditions whatever seemed to them of a nature to support their spiritual views as well as their material interests, and that they constructed therefrom not only what has come down to us as the four canonical gospels, but also the whole edifice of Christian dogma.

Consequently, we need not be surprised to find in the *New Testament* only unimportant fragments dealing with reincarnation; but even these are not to be despised, for they prove that the doctrine was, to a certain extent at all events, known and accepted in Palestine.

Reincarnation in the Gospels.

Saint Mark, Chapter 6.

v. 14. And King Herod heard of him; and he said, That John

the Baptist was risen from the dead....

v. 15. Others said, That it is Elias; and others said, That it is a prophet, or as one of the prophets.

v. 16. But when Herod heard thereof, he said, It is John whom I beheaded; he is risen from the dead.

Saint Matthew, Chapter 14.

v. 1. At that time, Herod the tetrarch heard of the fame of Jesus.

v. 2. And said unto his servants, This is John the Baptist; he is risen from the dead....

Saint Luke, Chapter 9.

v. 7. Now Herod the tetrarch heard of all that was done by him; and he was perplexed because it was said of some that John was risen from the dead.

v. 8. And of some, that Elias had appeared; and of others, that one of the old prophets was risen again.

v. 9. But Herod said, John have I beheaded; but who is this of whom I hear such things?

The account here given proves that the people as well as Herod believed in reincarnation, and that it applied, at all events, "to the prophets" and to those like them.

Saint Matthew, Chapter 16.

v. 13. When Jesus came into the coasts of Caesarea Philippi, he asked his disciples, saying, Whom do men say that I, the

Son of man, am?

v. 14. And they said, Some say that thou art John the Baptist; some, Elias; and others, Jeremias, or one of the prophets.

The same account is given in *Saint Luke*, chapter 9, verses 18, 19.

Saint Matthew, Chapter 17.

v. 12. But I say unto you, That Elias is come already, and they knew him not, but have done unto him whatsoever they listed. Likewise shall also the Son of man suffer of them.

v. 13. Then the disciples understood that he spake unto them of John the Baptist.

He continued in *Saint Matthew*, Chapter 11.

v. 7. Jesus began to say unto the multitudes concerning John, What went ye out into the wilderness to see? A reed shaken with the wind?

v. 8. But what went ye out for to see? A man clothed in soft raiment? Behold, they that wear soft clothing are in kings' houses.

v. 9. But what went ye out for to see? A prophet? Yea, I say unto you, and more than a prophet.

v. 14. And if ye will receive it, this is Elias which was for to come.

Here we have a distinct declaration: Reincarnation is a fact; John is the rebirth of Elias.[169]

Judging from these texts, one might be tempted to think that reincarnation was confined to the prophets or to people of importance, but Saint John shows us that the Jews, though perhaps ignorant that it was a law of universal application, recognised, at any rate, that it might happen in the case of any man.

Saint John, Chapter 9.

v. 1. And as Jesus passed by, he saw a man which was blind from his birth.

v. 2. And his disciples asked him, saying: Master, who did sin, this man or his parents, that he was born blind?

v. 3. Jesus answered, Neither hath this man sinned nor his parents; but that the works of God should be made manifest in him.

Here we are dealing with a man *blind from birth*, and the Jews ask Jesus if he was blind because he sinned; this clearly indicates that they were referring to sins committed in the course of a former existence[170]; the thought is, therefore, quite a natural, straightforward one, referring to something well known to everyone and needing no explanation.

As one well acquainted with this doctrine of Rebirth, without combating it as an error or as something doubtful which his disciples ought not to believe, Jesus simply replies:

"Neither hath this man sinned nor his parents; but that the works of God should be made manifest in him."

And yet it appears as though this answer must have been distorted, as so many others have been, otherwise it would mean that the only reason for this man's blindness was the caprice of the Deity.

Reincarnation in the Apocalypse.

The *Apocalypse*, an esoteric book *par excellence*, confirms the doctrine of Reincarnation, and throws considerable light on it:

"Him that overcometh will I make a pillar in the temple of my God, and he shall go no more out...."[171]

In another verse it is stated that to him who overcometh "I will give the morning star."[172] In the language of theosophy, this means: He who has overcome the animal soul, shall, by mystic Communion, be united to the divine soul, which, in the *Apocalypse*, is the symbol of the Christ:

"I, Jesus, am the bright and morning star."[173]

Another verse clearly characterises the nature and the cost of victory:

"To him that overcometh will I give to eat of the hidden manna, and I will give him a *white stone*, and in the stone a new *name* written, which no man knoweth saving he that receiveth it."[174]

The hidden manna is the ambrosia of the Greeks, the *kyteon* of the mysteries of Eleusis, the *soma* of the Hindus, the eucharist of the Christians, the sacred drink offered to the disciples at Initiation, which had the Moon as its symbol, conferred the gift of divine clairvoyance and separated the soul from the body.

The "white stone" is none other than the *alba petra*, the white cornelian, the chalcedony, or stone of Initiation. It was given to the candidate who had successfully passed through all the preliminary tests.[175] The "Word" written on the stone is the *sacred Word*, the "lost Word" which Swedenborg said was to be sought for amongst the hierophants of Tartary and Tibet, whom theosophists call the Masters.

"He who overcometh" is, therefore, the disciple ready for initiation; it is of him that "a pillar in the temple of God" will be made. In esoteric language, the column signifies Man redeemed, made divine and free, who is no longer to revolve on the wheel of Rebirths, who "shall no more go out," as the *Apocalypse* says, *i.e.*, shall not again leave Heaven.

If we examine the text of both *Old* and *New Testament* by the light of esoteric teaching, the dead letter, often absurd and at tunes repellent and immoral, would receive unexpected illumination, and would fully justify the words of the great rabbi, Maimonides, quoted a few pages back.[176]

Origen, the most learned of the Fathers of the Church, adds in his turn:

"If we had to limit ourselves to the letter, and understand after the fashion of the Jews or the people, what is written in the Law, I should be ashamed to proclaim aloud that it was God who gave us such laws; I should find more dignity and reason in human laws, as, for instance, in those of Athens, Rome, or Sparta...." (*Homil 7. in Levit.*)

Saint Jerome, in his *Epistle to Paulinus*, continues in similar fashion:

"Listen, brother, learn the path you must follow in studying the Holy Scriptures. Everything you read in the divine books is shining and light-giving without, but far sweeter is the heart thereof. He who would eat the nut must first break the shell."

It is because they have lost the Spirit of their Scriptures that the Christians—ever since their separation from the Gnostics—have offered the world nothing more than the outer shell of the World Religion.

NEOPLATONISM

The great philosophic body that formed a bridge, as it were, between the Old World and the New was the famous School of Alexandria, founded about the second century of our era by Ammonius Saccas and closed in the year 429 A.D. through the intolerance of Justinian. Theosophical in its origin, this school had received from Plato the esoteric teaching of Egypt and the East, and the dogma of Rebirth was secretly taught in its entirety, though its meaning may have been travestied by the ignorance of the masses to whom only the grosser aspects of the teaching were given.

"It is a dogma recognised throughout antiquity," says Plotinus,[177] "that the soul expiates its sins in the darkness of the infernal regions, and that afterwards it passes into new bodies, there to undergo new trials."

"When we have gone astray in multiplicity,[178] we are first punished by our wandering away from the path, and afterwards by less favourable conditions, when we take on new bodies."[179]

"The gods are ever looking down upon us in this world, no reproach we bring against them can be justifiable, for their providence is never-ending; they allot to each individual his appropriate destiny, one that is in harmony with his past conduct, in conformity with his successive existences."[180]

The following is a quotation from the same philosopher, dealing with metempsychosis, and which, when compared with the foregoing sentences, appears strangely absurd. We make no comment here, as this obscure question will be dealt with a few pages farther on.

"Those who have exercised human faculties are reborn as men; those who have lived only the life of the senses pass into animals' bodies, especially into the bodies of wild beasts if they have given way to excesses of anger ... those who have sought only to satisfy their lust and gluttony, pass into the bodies of lascivious and gluttonous animals ... those who have allowed their senses to become atrophied, are sent to vegetate in trees ... those who have reigned tyranically become eagles, if they have no other vice."[181]

Porphyry says:

"The souls that are not destined for the tortures of hell (*Tartarus*), and those that have passed through this expiation, are born again, and divine Justice gives them a new body, in accordance with their merits and demerits."[182]

The following remarkable lines are from Iamblichus:

"What appears to us to be an accurate definition of justice does not also appear to be so to the Gods. For we, looking at that which is most brief, direct our attention to things present, and to this momentary life, and the manner in which it subsists. But the powers that are superior to us know the whole life of the Soul, and all its former lives; and, in consequence of this, if they inflict a certain punishment in obedience to the entreaties of those that invoke them, they do not inflict it without justice, but looking at the offences committed by souls in former lives: which men, not perceiving, think that they unjustly fall into the calamities which they suffer."[183]

Proclus gave out the same teaching; he affirmed that he had been incarnated in Nichomachus, the Pythagorean.

In his commentary on the *Golden Verses of Pythagoras*, Hierocles expresses himself thus:

"The ways of the Lord can be justified only by metempsychosis."[184]

Damascius and Hermias, as also their masters, proclaimed their belief in Rebirth.

Here a short explanation must be given of what has been said regarding transmigration or metempsychosis, in order that all misunderstanding may be removed.

Neither Pythagoras nor Plotinus nor any of the great Teachers of the past believed in metempsychosis, as it has been described; all their disciples have affirmed if, and these affirmations, set over against a line of teaching which seems to contradict them, because it is incomplete and intended for the less intelligent portion of society at that time, ought to have reminded its opponents that there might be hidden reasons capable of explaining the paradox.

We must first remember that a veil of strictest secrecy was flung over the noblest and most sublime spiritual teachings of the day. According to Bossuet, the teaching of the immortality of the soul seems not to have been deemed suitable for the Hebrew race, and, indeed, it is easy to understand that no double-edged truth should be taught except under conditions that would safeguard it. Ptolemy Philadelphus exiled Hegesias,[185] whose eloquent fanaticism had caused some of his disciples to commit suicide, at Cyrene, after a lesson on immortality. Ptolemy ordered those schools of philosophy to be closed which continued teaching this doctrine, for in the case of a people insufficiently developed, the instinct which binds to physical life, and the dread of the torture that awaits guilty souls in the Hereafter, are preferable to doctrines of immortality deprived of the safeguards with which they should be surrounded.

The doctrine of Rebirths called for even stricter secrecy than that of immortality, and this secrecy was accorded it in ancient times; after the coming of the Christ, it grew less rigorous, and the Neoplatonists, though obliged to keep the esoteric teaching to themselves, were permitted to throw light on certain points.

Timaeus of Locris, one of the masters of Plotinus, hinted at the existence of a more profound doctrine in the following words:

"Just as by the threat of punishment imperfectly evolved souls are prevented from sinning, so the transmigration of the souls of murderers into the bodies of wild beasts, and of the souls of unchaste persons into the bodies of swine, was taught; and the previous punishment of these souls in the infernal regions was entrusted to Nemesis (Karma)."

Certain modern commentators—though imperfectly instructed in the teachings of palingenesis—have also seen that the masters of philosophy in the past could not possibly have made a mistake which less far-seeing minds would have avoided. Dacier[186] says:

"A sure token that Pythagoras never held the opinion attributed to him lies in the fact that there is not the faintest trace of it in the symbols we have left of him, or in the precepts his disciple, Lysis, collected together and handed down as a summary of the master's teachings."

Jules Simon also speaks as follows regarding Plotinus:[187]

"Here we have the doctrine of metempsychosis which Plotinus found all around, among the Egyptians, the Jews, the Neoplatonists, his predecessors, and finally in Plato himself. Does Plato take metempsychosis seriously, as one would be tempted to believe after reading the *Republic*? Did he mention it only to ridicule the superstitions of his contemporaries, as seems evident from the *Timaeus*?[188]

"However important Plato may have considered metempsychosis, it can scarcely be imagined that Plotinus took it seriously.... Even granting that this doctrine were literally accepted by Plotinus, the question would still have to be asked whether the human soul really does dwell in the body of an animal, or simply enters a human body, which, in its passions and vices, recalls the nature of that particular animal."

The reasons mentioned by Dacier and Jules Simon form only a trifling portion of the whole explanation, but if they are added to the constant protests raised by the disciples of the Masters of the Pythagorean and Platonic traditions, against those who said that their instructors taught metempsychosis in all its crudeness, they assume considerable importance, and show that, although the restrictions of esoteric teaching travestied by the ignorance of the masses may have caused it to be believed that the contrary was the case, none the less the Initiates, from the very beginning, denied that human transmigration into the bodies of animals ever took place.

On this question many of them have frequently said that it is the soul which, in such cases, changes its nature, and assumes the passions of animals into which, as is said exoterically, it transmigrates, though it does not enter into their bodies.

"He who believes that he transmigrates, after death, into the body of a beast or a plant," says Hierocles,[189] "is grossly mistaken; he is ignorant of the fact that the essential form of the soul cannot change, that it is and it remains human, and only, metaphorically speaking, does virtue make of it a god, and vice an animal."

"A human soul," adds Hermes, "cannot go back into the body of an animal; it is preserved from such pollution, for all time, by the will of the gods."[190]

Mrs. Besant says as follows in a letter dealing with Theosophy and Reincarnation (*The Theosophist*, April, 1906):

"Even with the wealth of detail given in the Hindu Shastras, thousands of facts of the invisible world are omitted, because their statement would hopelessly bewilder the public mind.

"If all the details are given, ere the main principles are grasped, hopeless confusion is caused to the beginner."

"When an Ego, a human soul, by vicious appetite or otherwise, forms a very strong link of attachment to any type of animal, the astral body (Kamarupa) of such a person shows the corresponding animal characteristics, and in the astral world, where thoughts and passions are visible as forms, may take the animal shapes; thus, after death, in *Pretaloka*, the soul would be embodied in an animal vesture, resembling or approximating to the animal whose qualities had been encouraged during earth-life. Either at this stage, or when the soul is returning towards reincarnation, and is again in the astral world, it may, in extreme cases, be linked by magnetic affinity to the astral body of the animal it has approached in character, and will then, through the animal's astral body, be chained as a prisoner to that animal's physical body. Thus chained, it cannot go onwards to *Svarga*, if the tie be set up while it is a *Preta*; nor go onwards to human birth, if it be descending towards physical life. It is truly undergoing penal servitude, chained to an animal; it is conscious in the astral world, has its human faculties, but it cannot control the brute body with which it is connected, nor express itself through that body on the physical plane. The animal organisation does not possess the mechanism needed by the human Ego for self-expression; it can serve as a jailor, not as a vehicle. Further, the "animal soul" is not ejected, but is the proper tenant and controller of its own body. S'ri Shankaracharya hints very clearly at the difference between this penal imprisonment and becoming a stone, a tree, or an animal. Such an imprisonment is not "reincarnation," ... the human Ego "cannot reincarnate as an animal," cannot "become an animal."

"In cases where the Ego is not degraded enough for absolute imprisonment, but in which the astral body has become very animal, it may pass on normally to human re-birth, but the animal characteristic will be largely reproduced in the physical body—as witness the "monsters" who in face are sometimes repulsively animal, pig-faced, dog-faced, &c. Men, by yielding to the most bestial vices, entail on themselves penalties more terrible than they, for the most part, realise; for Nature's laws work on unbrokenly and bring to every man the harvest of the seed he sows. The suffering entailed on the conscious human entity, thus cut off from progress and from self-expression, is very great, and is, of course, reformatory in its action; it is somewhat similar to that endured by other Egos, who are linked to bodies human in form, but without normal brains—those we call idiots, lunatics, &c. Idiocy and lunacy are the results of vices different in kind from those that bring about the animal servitude above explained, but the Ego in these cases also is attached to a form through which he cannot express himself."

"True reason," says Proclus,[191] "affirms that the human soul may at times find lodgment in brutes, but that it is possible for it to live its own life and rise above the lower nature whilst bound to it by the similarity of its tendencies and desires. We have never meant anything else, as has often been proved by the reasoning in our commentaries on *Phaedrus*."

There is a note in the *Vahan*[192] on a passage from *Phaedrus* which sheds all the light that can be shed on the question of metempsychosis; in the space of a few lines everything is said that may be publicly revealed, without trespassing on forbidden ground.

After stating that, on returning from the internal regions, the soul passes into the "life" of a beast, and that if it were human previously, it afterwards goes into another human body, the note continues:

"We must not understand by this that the soul of a man becomes the soul of a brute, but that by way of punishment it is bound to the soul of a brute, or carried in it, just as daemons used to reside in our souls. Hence all the energies of the rational soul are absolutely impeded, and its intellectual eye beholds nothing but the dark and tumultuous phantasms of a brutal life."[193]

This passage contains the explanation of what might be called the metempsychosis of certain human souls at the present time; we once heard a great Teacher fully reveal this mystery to a chosen group of Hindus, but it must for some time to come remain a mystery to the western world. All that can be said on the matter is that it has nothing to do with the incarnation of a human soul in the body of an animal, but rather with a certain temporary karmic bond, in the life Hereafter, between a human soul and an animal one, a bond intended to teach many a hard lesson to the one who has brought upon himself so unpleasant an experience.

Metempsychosis included many other facts in human evolution, facts that were plainly taught to the disciples in the "inner circles" of the ancient Schools and passed out to the confused medley of public teaching.

The astral body, for instance, of a man of an exceedingly passionate nature, when the soul leaves the physical body, sometimes assumes forms resembling those of the animals which represent these passions on the physical plane, and so the disincarnate soul of an assassin has been said to pass into the body of a wild beast.

Metempsychosis, properly so-called, that is to say, the passing of a human soul into the body of a brute, did however exist during the infancy of the human race, when highly developed animal souls were becoming fit to enter the human kingdom. The bodies of these newly-born human souls were coarse and rudimentary in their nature, showing scarcely any difference in form and organic function from the bodies of the higher animals of that period, for these instruments were very similar to one another. The improvements subsequently effected by human bodies did not then exist; the difference, or distinction, which has now widened into a gulf, was scarcely perceptible, and in the early incarnations of these rudimentary human souls back-slidings and falls were so frequent that some of them, thus enfeebled, might find it to their advantage[194] to become incarnate, at times, in highly-developed animal bodies. But

Th. Pascal

that was always an exception, and the exception has long ago become an impossibility.

We think these explanations, along with those given in other portions of this work, will throw as much light as is permitted publicly on the subject of metempsychosis—a subject frequently discussed and one that has hitherto been so obscure. Such illumination as is here given is due to the teachings of theosophy.

THE EARLY CHRISTIAN CHURCH

The documents to which we have access, dealing with the philosophical and religious history of Christianity in the first few centuries of our era, are so questionable, that we can place but faint reliance upon them, if we would really become acquainted with the thought of that period. We have already seen that the number of spurious or counterfeit productions was so great that a strange kind of sorting out, or selection, took place at the first Council of Nicaea, resulting in the choice of four so-called canonical Gospels. It is evident, too, that the copyists, compilers, and translators of the period were anxious, above all else, to make facts and opinions agree with their preconceived ideas and personal sympathies or likings. Each author worked *pro domo sua*, emphasising whatever fitted in with his personal views and carefully concealing what was calculated to weaken them; so that at the present time the only clues we have to guide us out of the labyrinth consist of the brief opinions expressed by a few historians, here and there, on whose honesty reliance may be placed.

In the present chapter, for instance, it is no easy matter to unravel the Truth from out of these tangled threads of personal opinions. Some believe that the early Christians and the Fathers of the Church were reincarnationists; others say they were not; the texts, we are in possession of, contradict one another. Thus, whereas Saint Jerome brings against Origen the reproach of having in his book *De Principiis* taught that, in certain cases, the transmigration of human souls into the bodies of animals, was possible—as, indeed, seems to be the case—certain writers deny that he ever said anything on the subject. These contradictory affirmations are easy to explain, once we know that Ruffinus, when translating into Latin the Greek text of *De Principiis*, omitted all that referred to this question, that the conspiracy of silence might be preserved on the matter of Origenian transmigration.

At the close of his article "*Origen on Reincarnation*," in the *Theosophical Review*, February, 1906, G. R. S. Mead says:

"It therefore follows that those who have claimed Origen as a believer in reincarnation—and many have done so, confounding reincarnation with pre-existence—have been mistaken. Origen himself answers in no uncertain tones, and stigmatises the belief as a false doctrine, utterly opposed to Scripture and the teaching of the Church."

Others affirm that Saint Justin Martyr believed in rebirths and even in the transmigration of human souls into animal bodies. In his book *Against Heresies*, volume 2, chapter 33, the *Absurdity of the Doctrine of the Transmigration of Souls* is dealt with; and in the following chapter, the pre-existence of the soul is denied! Is this another instance, like the one just mentioned, of tampering with the writings of this Father of the Church?[195]

At times an author gives two contradictory opinions on the same subject. In Tertullian's *Apology for the Christians*, for instance, we find the following:

"If you can find it reasonable to believe the transmigration of human souls from body to body, why should you think it incredible for the soul to return to the substance it first inhabited?[196] For this is our notion of a resurrection, to be that again after death which we were before, for according to the Pythagorean doctrine these souls now are not the same they were, because they cannot be what they were not without ceasing to be what they were.... I think it of more consequence to establish this doctrine of the resurrection; and we propose it as more consonant with reason and the dignity of human nature to believe that man will be remade man, each person the person he was, a human being a human being; in other words, that the soul shall be habited with the same qualities it was invested with in its former union, though the man may receive some alteration in his form.... The light which daily departs rises again with its original splendour, and darkness succeeds by equal turns; the stars which leave the world, revive; the seasons, when they have finished their course, renew it again; the fruits are consumed and bloom afresh; and that which we sow is not quickened except it die, and by that dissolution rises more fruitful. Thus you see how all things are renewed by corruption and reformed by dying.... How, then, could you imagine that man, the lord of all these dying and reviving things, should himself die for ever?"

After such a clear and noble profession of faith, we may well wonder if it were the same man who, in *De Anima*, could have both refuted and pitilessly ridiculed the idea of rebirth, and denied the separation of the soul from the body as well as the influence of the former upon the latter. We prefer to believe that we are dealing with two writers, or else that some literary forger, anxious to create a diversion, deliberately made Tertullian responsible for this strange contradiction.

Another reason for the difficulty in unravelling the tangled skein of the religious and philosophical teachings prevalent in the early centuries of Christianity is the lack of precision in the language of the writers, the loss of the key to the special vocabulary they used, and the veils which writers who possessed some degree of initiation, deliberately threw over teachings which could only be given to the masses in general terms.

There is one very important point to consider; and this is that in the earlier centuries, outside the circles of initiation, there was not that precision which the present-day teaching of theosophy has given to the doctrine of Reincarnation; this latter, in the mind of the people, became confused with the doctrine of Pre-existence, which affirms that the soul exists before coming into the present body, and will exist in other bodies after leaving this one. This confusion has continued up to the present time, and we find schools of spiritualism in England and America, as well as in other countries, teaching that existence on earth has been preceded and will be followed by a great number of existences on the invisible planes.

In reality, this is the doctrine of Rebirths, though there is nothing precise about the teaching. Whether the soul has a single physical body, or takes several in succession, it is none the less continually evolving as it passes into material vehicles, however subtle the matter be; the difference is, therefore, insignificant, unless we wish to enter into details of the process involved, as was the case in the West in the early centuries of Christianity.

Did the Fathers of the Church teach Pre-existence? There can be no doubt on this point. In a letter to St. Anastasius, Rufinus said that "this belief was common amongst the early Christian fathers." Arnobius[197] shows his sympathy with this teaching, and adds that St. Clement, of Alexandria, "wrote wonderful accounts of metempsychosis"; and afterwards, in other passages of the same book, he appears to criticise the idea of the plurality of lives. St. Jerome affirms that "the doctrine of transmigration has been secretly taught from ancient times to small numbers of people, as a traditional truth which was not to be divulged."[198] A. Franck quotes this passage on page 184 of his *Kabbale*; Huet, too, gives it in *Origeniana*.[199] The same Father proves himself to be a believer in Pre-existence, in his 94th *Letter to Avitus*, where he agrees with Origen on the subject of the interpretation of a passage from St. Paul,[200] and says that this means "that a divine abode and true repose are to be found in Heaven," and "that there dwell creatures endowed with reason in a state of bliss, before coming down to our visible world, before they fall into the grosser bodies of earth...."

Lactantius, whom St. Jerome called the Christian Cicero, though he opposed pagan doctrines, maintained that the soul was capable of immortality and of bodily survival only on the hypothesis that it existed before the body.[201]

Nemesius, Bishop of Emissa in Syria, stoutly affirmed the doctrine of Pre-existence, declaring that every Greek who believed in immortality believed also in the pre-existence of the soul.

St. Augustine said: "Did I not live in another body, or somewhere else, before entering my mother's womb?"[202]

In his *Treatise, on Dreams*, Synesius states that "philosophy assures us that our past lives are a direct preparation for future lives...." When invited by the citizens of Ptolemais to become their bishop, he at once refused, saying that "he cherished certain opinions of which they might not approve, as, after mature reflection, they had struck deep root in his mind. Foremost among these, he mentioned the doctrine of Pre-existence."

Dr. Henry More, the famous Platonist of the seventeenth century, quotes Synesius as one of the masters who taught this doctrine,[203] and Beausobre reports a typical phrase of his,[204] "Father, grant that my soul may merge into Light and be no more thrust back into the illusion of earth."

St. Gregory of Nysa says it is absolutely necessary that the soul should be healed and purified, and if this does not take place during its life on earth, it must be accomplished in future lives.

St. Clement of Alexandria says that, although man was created after other beings, "the human species is more ancient than all these things."[205] In his *Exhortations to the Pagans*, he adds:

"We were in being long before the foundation of the world; we existed in the eye of God, for it is our destiny to live in him. We are the reasonable creatures of the divine Word; therefore, we have existed from the beginning, for in the beginning was the Word.... Not for the first time does He show pity on us in out wanderings. He pitied us from the very beginning."

He also adds:[205]

"Philolaus, the Pythagorean, taught that the soul was flung into the body as a punishment for the misdeeds it had committed, and his opinion was confirmed by the most ancient of the prophets."

As regards Reincarnation, *i.e.*, the descent of the human soul

Th. Pascal

into successive physical bodies, and even its temporary association with the physical bodies of animals, more than one Christian writer advocated this teaching.

Chalcidius, quoted by Beausobre in the book just mentioned, says:

"The souls, that are not able to unite with God, are destined to return to life until they repent of their misdeeds."

In the *Pistis Sophia*, a Christian treatise on the mysteries of the divine Hierarchies and the evolution of souls in the three worlds, we find the doctrine of Rebirth frequently mentioned:

"If he is a man who (after passing out of his body)[206] shall have come to the end of his cycles of transmigrations, without repenting, ... he is cast into outer darkness."

A few pages earlier, in the same work, we find:

"The disincarnate soul which has not solved the mystery of the breaking of the bonds and of the seals is brought before the virgin of light, who, after judging it, hands it over to her agents (*receivers*), who carry it into a new body."

Let us now see what Origen says on the matter[207]:

"Celsus, then, is altogether ignorant of the purpose of our writings, and it is therefore upon his own acceptation of them that he casts discredit and not upon their real meaning; whereas if he had reflected on what is appropriate[208] to a soul which is to enjoy an everlasting life, and on the idea which we are to form of its essence and principles, he would not so have ridiculed the entrance of the immortal into a mortal body, which took place, not according to the metempsychosis of Plato, but agreeably to another and higher order of things."

The teaching of Origen is not easy to set forth clearly, for he is very reticent about many things, and employs a language to which present-day philosophy cannot always find the key; still, the teaching seems full and complete. It comprises pre-existence and even those special associations of certain human souls with animal souls, which we have just spoken of and which form one of the chief mysteries of metempsychosis.

In the following words he explains the existence of souls in previous worlds:

"The soul has neither beginning nor end....

"Rational creatures existed undoubtedly from the very beginning in those (ages) which are invisible and eternal. And if this is so, then there has been a descent from a higher to a lower condition on the part not only of those souls who have deserved the change, by the variety of their movements, but also on that of those who, in order to serve the whole world, were brought down from those higher and invisible spheres to these lower and visible ones, although against their will. 'For the creature was made subject to vanity, not willingly, but by reason of him who hath subjected the same in hope' (*Rom.*, chap. 8, v. 20); so that both sun and moon and stars and angels might discharge their duly to the world, and to those souls who, on account of their excessive mental defects, stood in need of bodies of a grosser and more solid nature; and for the sake of those for whom this arrangement was necessary, this visible world was also called into being.

"This arrangement of things, then, which God afterwards appointed not being understood by some, who failed to perceive that it was owing to preceding causes originating in free will, that this variety of arrangement had been instituted by God, they have concluded that all things in this world are directed either by fortuitous movements or by a necessary fate, and that nothing is in the power of our own will."[209]

"Is it not rational that souls should be introduced into bodies, in accordance with their merits and previous deeds, and that those who have used their bodies in doing the utmost possible good should have a right to bodies endowed with qualities superior to the bodies of others?"[210]

All souls will arrive at the same goal;[211] it is the will of souls that makes of them angels, men or demons, and their fall can be of such a nature that they may be chained down to the bodies of animals.[212] Certain souls, on attaining to perfect peace, return to new worlds; some remain faithful, others degenerate to such a degree that they become demons.[213]

Concerning bodies, he says:

"The soul, which is immaterial and invisible in its nature, exists in no material place, without having a body suited to the nature of that place; accordingly, it at one time puts off one body which was necessary before, but which is no longer adequate in its changed state, and it exchanges it for a second."[214]

Although *metensomatosis* (re-embodiment of the soul), *i.e.*, the true teaching of Origen, was not clearly expounded, it considerably influenced the early Christian philosophers, and was favourably received up to the time of its condemnation by the Synod of Constantinople. It appeared in most of the sects of that time and in those of the following centuries: Simonians, Basilidians, Valentinians, Marcionites, Gnostics,

Manichaeans, Priscillianites, Cathari, Patarins, Albigenses, Bogomiles, &c....

Chivalry, too, in these ages of darkness and persecution, was an instrument for the dissemination of esoteric doctrines, including Reincarnation. The heart of this noble institution consisted of students of divine Wisdom, pure devoted souls who communicated with one another by means of passwords.

The Troubadours were their messengers of the sacred Teaching, which they skilfully concealed in their songs, carrying it from group to group, from sect to sect, in their wanderings. "Sons of the teachings of the Albigenses and of the Manichaean-Marcion tradition"[215] they kept alive belief in the rebirths of the soul, "Izarn the Monk," in his book *Historie d' un Heretique*,[216] apostrophised an Albigensian bishop in the following terms:

"Tell me what school it was in which you learnt that the spirit of man, after losing his body, passes into an ox, an ass, a sheep, or a fowl, and transmigrates from one animal to another, until a new human body is born for it?"

Izarn was acquainted with only so much of the teachings of the Troubadours as had got abroad and been distorted and misrepresented by ignorant or evil-minded persons; still, his criticism plainly shows traces of the teachings of palingenesis in the darkest and most blood-stained periods of the Middle Ages.

The Inquisition put an end to the Troubadours, though certain of them, Dante and St. Francis of Assisi, for instance, by reason of their popularity or the special circumstances of the case, were left in peace. In Europe the secret teaching was continued by the Rosicrucians; the *Roman de la Rose* is pure Hermetic esotericism. The struggle of official Christianity—that of the letter—against those who represented the spirit of the Scriptures, raged ever more bitterly, and the idea of Rebirth disappeared more and more from the Church; its sole representatives during the Middle Ages were St. Francis of Assisi, the learned Irish monk, Johannes Scotus Erigena, and St. Bonaventura, "the Seraphic Doctor." At the present time there remains nothing more than a disfigured and misunderstood fragment of this idea: the dogma of the *Resurrection of the Body*.

ISLAMISM.[217]

It has been said that the Arabs believed in Reincarnation before Mohammed forbade it. Some, however, think that the Koran was written only after the death of the Prophet, and that the latter committed nothing to writing, but taught by word of mouth. Besides, it is clear that Mohammedanism is an offshoot of Zoroastrianism and Christianity. Like these, it teaches the Unity of the Whole, the divine Presence in all creatures and things (*Ubiquity*), Predestination, which is only one form of *Karma*, and Resurrection, which expresses one phase of Palingenesis.

Mohammed, like all great mystics, had discovered or learnt many of the truths of esotericism. The verses of the Koran that refer to the "Companions of the Cave"[218] indicate that he knew more than he taught in public, and that there may be some ground for certain Asiatic nations holding the exaggerated belief that he was an Avatar,[219] the tenth incarnation of the *Aum*—the Amed, the Nations' Desire.[220] He was a Disciple.

Had there not been in the heart of Islamism a strong germ of esoteric teaching, Sufism could never have sprung from it. The Sufis are the saints of Mohammedanism, they are those who aspire after the union of the individual "I" with the cosmic "I," of man with God; they are frequently endowed with wonderful powers, and their chiefs have almost always been thaumaturgists.

The *New Koran*, a modern exposition of part of the secret doctrine of Islam, shows the correctness of this view. In it we find the following passages on the subject of Palingenesis:

"And when his body falleth off altogether, as an old fish-shell, his soul doeth welt by the releasing, and formeth a new one instead."

"The disembodied spirits of man and beast return as the clouds to renew the young streamlets of infancy....

"When a man dieth or leaveth his body, he wendeth through the gate of oblivion and goeth to God, and when he is born again he cometh from God and in a new body maketh his dwelling; hence is this saying:

"The body to the tomb and the spirit to the womb....

"This doctrine is none other than what God hath taught openly from the very beginning....

"For truly the soul of a man goeth not to the body of a beast, as some say....

"But the soul of the lower beast goeth to the body of the higher, and the soul of the higher beast to the body of the savage, and the soul of the savage to the man....

"And so a man shall be immortal in one body and one

garment that neither can fade nor decay."

"Ye who now lament to go out of this body, wept also when ye were born into it...."[221]

"The person of man is only a mask which the soul putteth on for a season; it weareth its proper time and then is cast off, and another is worn in its stead....

"I tell you, of a truth, that the spirits which now have affinity shall be kindred together, although they all meet in new persons and names."[222]

In *Asiatic Researches*, Colebrooke states that the present Mohammedan sect of the *Bohrahs* believes in metempsychosis, as do the Hindus, and, like the latter, abstains from flesh, for the same reason.

Thus we find the doctrine of Reincarnation at the heart of all the great religions of antiquity. The reason it has remained in a germinal state in recent religions—Christianity and Islamism—is that in the latter Mohammed did not attain to the degree of a Hierophant, and in all likelihood the race to which he brought light did not greatly need to become acquainted with the law relating to the return to earth life; whereas in the former the real teachings of the Christ were lost when the Gnostics were exterminated, and Eusebius and Irenaeus, the founders of exoteric Christianity, unable to grasp the *spirit*, imposed the *letter* throughout the religion.

THE DOCTRINE OF REBIRTH IN MODERN PHILOSOPHY

In antiquity, science and philosophy were scarcely anything

else than parts of religion[223]; the most eminent scientists and the greatest philosophers alike were all supporters of the established form of religion, whenever they did not happen to be its priests, for the temples were the common cradle of science and philosophy. No wonder, then, that we find these three great aspects of Truth always hand in hand, never opposed to or in conflict with one another through the whole of antiquity. Science was for the body, philosophy for the intellect, and religion for that divine spark which is destined to flash forth and finally become a "god" in the bosom of the World Soul. Every intelligent man knew that on this tripod lay the life of the individual, the life of society, and the life of the world. Divorce between these took place only at a later date, when the divine Teachers had disappeared, and mutilated traditions handed down to the nations nothing but disfigured and incomplete teachings buried beneath the ruins of temples that had been crumbling away ever since spiritual Life had left them.

Then followed the era of separation; science and philosophy became debased and went their own ways, whilst a degenerate religion reflected nothing higher than the narrow mentality of fallen ministers. As this degradation continued, there sprang into being religious wars, monstrosities that were unknown in those times when Divinity shed illumination and guidance on the nations by means of those mighty souls, the Adept-Kings: gods, demi-gods, and heroes.

Nevertheless, Truth never remained without her guardians, and when apostleship had been destroyed by persecutions the sacred treasure which was to be handed down from age to age was secretly entrusted by the sages to faithful disciples. Thus did Esoterism pass through fire and bloodshed, and one of its greatest teachings, the doctrine of Palingenesis, has left a stream of light in its wake. Now we will give a rapid sketch of it in modern times, examining the philosophical teachings of the greatest of recent thinkers. We will borrow mainly from Walker's work on this subject, quoting only the writers most deserving of mention, and making only short extracts, for all that is needed is to plant a few sign-posts to guide the student along the path.

In the 128th verse of *Lalla Rookh*, Thomas Moore speaks of rebirths:

"Stranger, though new the frame
Thy soul inhabits now, I've traced its flame
For many an age, in every chance and change
Of that Existence, through whose varied range,—
As through a torch-race, where, from hand to hand
The flying youths transmit their shining brand,—
From frame to frame the unextinguished soul
Rapidly passes, till it reach the goal!"

Paracelsus, like every Initiate, was acquainted with it, and Jacob Boehme, the "nursling of the Nirmanakayas,"[224] knew that it was a law of Nature.

Giordano Bruno—also a great Soul—quotes from Ovid's *Metamorphoses*, Book 15, Line 156, &c., as follows:

"O mortals! chilled by dreams of icy death,
Whom air-blown bubbles of a poet's breath,
Darkness and Styx in error's gulph have hurl'd,
With fabled terrors of a fabled world;
Think not, whene'er material forms expire,
Consumed by wasting age or funeral fire,
Aught else can die: souls, spurning death's decay,
Freed from their old, new tenements of clay
Forthwith assume, and wake to life again.
                    ... All is change,
Nought perishes" ...

Campanella, the Dominican monk, was sent into exile on account of his belief in the successive returns of the soul to earth.

The Younger Helmont, in his turn, was attacked by the inquisition for leaching this doctrine in his *De Revolutione Animarum*, in which he brings forward, in two hundred problems, all the arguments; that make reincarnation necessary.

Cudworth and Dr. Henry More, the Platonists of Cambridge, were faithful believers in Palingenesis; whilst Joseph Glanvill, in *Lux Orientalis*, finds that there are "Seven Pillars" on which Pre-existence rests.

Dr. Edward Beecher, in *The Conflict of Ages* and *The Concord of Ages*, as well as Julius Muller, the well-known German theologian, in *The Christian Doctrine of Sin*, warmly uphold it.

Schelling acknowledges it in his *Dissertation on Metempsychosis*.

Leibnitz, in his *Monadology*, and more especially his *Theodicy*, witnessed to his belief in this doctrine. Had he dared to speak out his thoughts openly, he would more effectively have advocated his "Optimism," by the teachings of evolution and rebirths, than by all the other arguments he advanced.

Chevalier Ramsey, in *The Philosophical Principles of Natural and Revealed Religion*, writes:

"The holy oracles always represent Paradise as our native

country, and our present life as an exile. How can we be said to have been banished from a place in which we never were? This argument alone would suffice to convince us of pre-existence, if the prejudice of infancy inspired by the schoolmen had not accustomed us to look upon these expressions as metaphorical, and to believe, contrary to Scripture and reason, that we were exiled from a happy state, only for the fault and personal disobedience of our first parents....

"Our Saviour seems to approve the doctrine of pre-existence in his answer to the disciples, when they interrogate him thus about the man born blind,[226] 'Master, who did sin, this man or his parents, that he was born blind?' It is clear that this question would have been ridiculous and impertinent if the disciples had not believed that the man born blind had sinned before his corporal birth, and consequently that he had existed in another state long ere he was born on earth. Our Saviour's answer is remarkable, 'Neither hath this man sinned nor his parents, but that the works of God might be manifested in him.' Jesus Christ could not mean that neither this man nor his parents had ever committed any sin, for this can be said of no mortal; but the meaning is that it was neither for the sins committed by this man in a state of pre-existence, nor for those of his parents, that he was born blind; but that he was deprived of sight from his birth, by a particular dispensation of Providence, in order to manifest, one day, the power of God in our Saviour. Our Lord, therefore, far from blaming and redressing this error in his disciples, as he did those concerning his temporal kingdom, answers in a way that seems to suppose with them, and confirm them in the doctrine of pre-existence. If he had looked upon this opinion as a capital error, would it have been consonant or compatible with his eternal wisdom to have passed it over so lightly and thus tacitly authorised it by such silence? On the contrary, does not his silence manifestly indicate that he looked upon this doctrine, which was a received maxim of the Jewish Church, as the true explanation of original sin?

"Since God says that he loved Jacob and detested Esau ere they were born, and before they had done good or evil in this mortal life, since God's love and hatred depend upon the moral dispositions of the creature, ... it follows clearly that if God hated Esau, type of the reprobate, and loved Jacob, type of the elect, before their natural birth, they must have pre-existed in another state.

"If it be said that all these texts are obscure, that pre-existence is largely drawn from them by induction, and that this belief is not revealed in Scripture by express words, I answer that the doctrines of the immortality of the soul are nowhere revealed, least of all in the oracles of the *Old* and *New Testament*. We may say the same of pre-existence. This doctrine is nowhere expressly revealed as an article of faith, but it is evidently implied in the *Wisdom of Solomon*, by the author of *Ecclesiasticus*, by our Saviour's silence, by St. Paul's comparisons, and by the sacred doctrine of original sin, which becomes not only inexplicable, but absurd, repugnant, and impossible, if that of pre-existence be not true.... The Fifth General Council held at Constantinople pronounces anathema against all those who maintain the fabulous doctrine of pre-existence in the Origenian sense. It was not then the simple doctrine of pre-existence that was condemned by the council, but the fictitious mixtures and erroneous disguises by which this ancient tradition had been adulterated by the Origenites."

Soame Jenyns writes:

"That mankind had existed in some state previous to the present was the opinion of the wisest sages of the most remote antiquity. It was held by the Gymnosophists of Egypt, the Brahmans of India, the Magi of Persia, and the greatest philosophers of Greece and Rome; it was likewise adopted by the *Fathers of the Christian Church, and frequently enforced by her early writers*; why it has been so little noticed, so much overlooked rather than rejected, by the divines and metaphysicians of latter ages, I am at a loss to account for, as it is undoubtedly confirmed by reason, by all the appearances of nature and the doctrines of revelation.

"In the first place, then, it is confirmed by reason, which teaches us that it is impossible that the conjunction of a male and female can create an immortal soul; they may prepare a material habitation for it; but there cannot be an immortal, pre-existent inhabitant ready to take possession. Reason assures us that an immortal soul, which will exist eternally after the dissolution of the body, must have eternally existed before the formation of it; *for whatever has no end can never have had any beginning*....

"Reason likewise tells us that an omnipotent and benevolent Creator would never have formed such a world as this, and filled it with such inhabitants if the present was the only, or even the first, state of their existence; for this state which, if unconnected with the past and the future, would seem calculated for no purpose intelligible to our understanding, neither of good or evil, of happiness or misery, of virtue or vice, of reward or punishment; but a confused jumble of them all together, proceeding from no visible cause and tending to no end....

"Pre-existence, although perhaps it is nowhere in the *New Testament* explicitly enforced, yet throughout the whole tenour of these writings is everywhere implied; in them, mankind is constantly represented as coming into the world under a load of guilt; as condemned criminals, the children of wrath and objects of divine indignation; placed in it for a time by the mercies of God to give them an opportunity of expiating this guilt by sufferings, and regaining, by a pious and virtuous conduct, their lost state of happiness and innocence....

"Now if by all this a pre-existent state is not constantly supposed, that is, that mankind has existed in some state previous to the present, in which this guilt was incurred, and this depravity contracted, there can be no meaning at all or such a meaning as contradicts every principle of common sense, that guilt can be contracted without acting, or that we can act without existing...."

The following is a quotation from Hume, the great positivist philosopher:

"Reasoning from the common course of nature, what is incorruptible must also be ingenerable. The soul, therefore, if immortal, existed before our birth, and if the former existence in noway concerned us, neither will the latter.... Metempsychosis is, therefore, the only system of this kind that philosophy can hearken to." (*The Immortality of the Soul.*)

Young, in his *Night Thoughts* (Night the Sixth), has the following lines:

"Look nature through, 'tis revolution all;
All change, no death. Day follows night; and night
The dying day; stars rise, and set, and rise;
Earth takes th' example ...

... All, to reflourish, fades;
As in a wheel, all sinks, to re-ascend.
Emblems of man, who passes, not expires."

"It is not more surprising to be born twice than once; everything in Nature is resurrection," said Voltaire.

Delormel, Descartes, and Lavater were struck with the tremendous importance of the doctrine of Palingenesis.

The Philosophy of the Universe, of Dupont de Nemours, is full of the idea of successive lives, as a necessary corollary of the law of progress; whilst Fontenelle strongly advocates it in his *Entretiens sur la Pluralite des Mondes*.

It is needless to state that these ideas formed part of the esoteric teachings of Martinez Pasqualis, Claude Saint-Martin, and their followers.

Saint-Martin lived in times that were too troubled for him to speak freely. In his works, however, not a few passages are found in which there can be no doubt that reincarnation is hinted at, to anyone able to read between the lines. (*Tableau nat.*, vol. I, p. 136; *L'homme de Desir*, p. 312.)

In his *Oeuvres Posthumes* (vol. I, p. 286) appears this remarkable passage:

"Death ought to be looked upon only as one stage in our journey. We reach this stage with tired, worn-out horses, and we start again with horses that are fresh and able to take us farther on our road; all the same, we must pay what we owe for the portion of the journey that has been traversed, and until the account is settled, we are not allowed to continue our way."

Goethe writes as follows to his friend Madame von Stein:

"Tell me what destiny has in store for us? Wherefore has it bound us so closely to each other? Ah! in bygone times, thou must have been my sister or my wife ... and there remains, from the whole of those past ages, only one memory, hovering like a doubt above my heart, a memory of that truth of old that is ever present in me."

Ballanche, an orthodox Christian mystic, says:

"Each one of us is a reincarnating being, ignorant both of his present and of his former transformations." (*Pal. Sociale*, book III., p. 154.)

"Man is brought to perfection only by becoming a more perfect order of things, and even then he does nothing more than bring back, as Plato said, a confused memory of the state that preceded his fall." (*Essai sur les Instit. Sociales*, vol. ii., p. 170.)

"This life we spend on earth, shut in between an apparent birth and an equally apparent death, is, in reality, only a portion of our existence, one manifestation of man in time." (*Orphee*, vol. iv., p. 424.)

"Our former lives belong to astronomical cycles lost in the mighty bosom of previous ages; not yet has it been given to us to know them." (*Orphee*, vol. iv., p. 432.)

Balzac's *Seraphita* abounds with references to the idea of successive lives:

"All human beings spend their first life in the sphere of instincts, in which they endeavour to discover how useless are the treasures of earth."

".... How often we live in this first world...."

"Then we have other existences to wear out before we reach

the path on which the light shines. Death is one stage on this journey."

Constant Savy[227] describes as follows the conditions of immortality and a succession of lives by means of reincarnation:

"In proportion as its soul is developed by successive lives, the body to which it is to be united will necessarily be superior to those it has worn out; otherwise there would be no harmony between these two elements of human existence; the means given to the soul would bear no relation to the development of its power. This body, gifted with more perfect and numerous senses, could not have an equal value for all....

"Besides, these natural inequalities are also advantageous for individual progress in another way; the errors resulting therefrom cause truths to be discovered; vices laid bare almost form a reason for the practice of virtue by all men, or at all events they protect one from vice by reason of the horror they inspire; the ignorance of some arouses the love of science in others; the very idleness which dishonours some men inspires others with a love for work."

"So that these inequalities, inevitable because they are necessary, are present in the successive lives we pass through. There is nothing in them contrary to universal harmony; rather, they are a means for effecting this harmony, and are the inevitable result of the difference in value that bodies possess. Besides, no man remains stationary; all advance at a more or less rapid rate of progress....

"When faith is born, it is an illumination. Since man's immortality is one progressive advance, and, to effect this, he prepares the life he enters by the life he is leaving; since, in short, there are necessarily two worlds, one material, the other intellectual, these two worlds, which make up the life to come, must be in harmonious relationship with our own.

"Man's work will, therefore, be a continuation of his past work....

"I would never believe that our intelligence, which begins to develop in this life, comes to a halt after such an imperfect growth, and is not exercised or perfected after death....

"... Nature always advances, always labours, because God is life and he is eternal, and life is the progressive movement in the direction of the supreme good, which is God himself. Could man alone in the whole of nature, man so imperfect and full of faults, stop in his onward course, either to be annihilated, or suddenly, without participating in it, though he was created free, find that he was as perfect as he could possibly be? This is more than I can understand.

"No, when the time comes, man will not find that his life has been useless, a thing for mere contemplation; he will not find that he is improved without personal participation therein, without effort and toil on his part; above all, he will not be reduced to a state of nothingness. He will again have a life of toil; he will participate, to the extent God has permitted him, in the endless creations produced by divine omnipotence; he will again love, he will never cease to love; he will continue his eternal progress, because the distance between himself and God is infinite."

Pierre Leroux says:

"If God, after creating the world and all creation, were then to abandon them, instead of guiding them from life to life, from one state of progress to another, to a goal of real happiness, he would be an unjust God. It is unnecessary for St. Paul to say; 'Shall the thing formed say to him that formed it. Why hast thou made me thus?' (*Romans*, chap, 9, v. 20.) There is an inner voice, doubtless coming to us from God himself, which tells us that God cannot bring about evil, or create in order to cause suffering. Now this is what would certainly happen were God to abandon his creatures after an imperfect, a truly unhappy life.

"On the other hand, if we regard the world as a series of successive lives for each creature, we see very well how it comes about that God, to whom there is neither time nor space, and who perceives the final goal of all things, permits evil and suffering as being necessary phases through which creatures must pass, in order to reach a state of happiness which the creature does not see, and, consequently, cannot enjoy in so far as it is a creature, but which God sees, and which, therefore, the creature virtually enjoys in him, for the time will come when it will partake of that happiness."[228]

In Fourier we find the following lines[229]:

"Where is there an old man who would not like to feel certain that he would be born again and bring back into another life the experience he has gained in the present one? To affirm that this desire cannot be realised is to confess that God is capable of deceiving us. We must, therefore, recognise that we have already lived before being what we now are, and that many another life awaits us, some in this world, and the rest in a higher sphere, with a finer body and more delicate senses...."

Alphonse Esquiros expresses himself as follows[230]:

"The question may well be asked whether the talents, the good and the evil tendencies man brings with him at birth may not be the fruit of acquired intelligence, of qualities and vices gained in one or many former existences. Is there a previous life the elements of which have prepared the conditions of the life now being lived by each of us? People in ancient times thought so. Inborn dispositions, so different in children, caused them to believe in impressions left by previous existences in the imperishable germ of man. From the time when intelligence begins to show itself in children we faintly discern a general attitude towards things, which is very like a memory thereof. It would appear that, according to this system, no one is unconnected with the elements he introduces into life at each birth.

"All the same, rebirth in humanity constitutes no more than an initial circle of tests. When, after one or several incarnations, man has attained to the degree of perfection necessary to cause a change, he passes to another life, and, in another sphere, begins an existence of which we know nothing, though it is possible for us to regard it as linked to the present life by the closest of bonds....

"The limit to the progress man must have attained to, before entering upon another circle of tests in another sphere, is at present unknown to us; science and philosophy will doubtless succeed in determining this limit later on."

"They alone are reborn to earthly flesh who have in no way raised the immortal principle of their nature to a degree of perfection that will enable them to be reborn in glory....

"I affirm the perpetual union of the soul to organic bodies; these bodies succeed each other, being born from one another, and fitting themselves for the constitutive forms of the worlds traversed by the immortal ego in its successive existences. The principle of life, extended to divers evolutions of rebirth, is ever for the Creator nothing more than a continuation of one and the same state. God does not regard the duration of a being as limited to the interval between birth and death; he includes all possible segments of existence, the succession of which, after many interruptions and renewals, forms the real unity of life. Must souls, when they leave our globe, put on, from sphere to sphere, an existence hidden from us, whose organic elements would continually be fitting themselves for the characters and natures of the different worlds? Reason can come to no decision on this point. Only let us not forget that the soul always carries off a material germ from one existence to the next, making itself anew, so to speak, several times, in that endless ascent of lives through the worlds, wherein it attains, heaven after heaven, a degree of perfection increasingly linked with the eternal elements of our growing personality.

"It may be seen, from what is here stated, how vain is the hypothesis of perfect bliss following on the death of the righteous.

"It is useless for the Christian to soar beyond time, beyond some limit that separates him from infinite good; he cannot do this by a single effort. God proportions his intervention and aid to the totality of the states man must pass through in the course of an indefinitely long series of existences...."

M. d'Orient, an orthodox Catholic, writes as follows[231]:

"In this doctrine, so evidently based on reason, everything is linked and held together: the foreknowledge of God and the agreement thereof with man's free-will. This problem, hitherto impossible to solve, no longer offers any difficulty, if by it is meant that God, knowing before birth, by reason of his previous deeds, what there is in the heart of man, brings man to life and removes him from it in circumstances that best fit in with the accomplishment of his purposes....

"We see in this way how it is that God is the controller of all the main events that take place in the world, for the knowledge he has of souls in former lives, and his power to dispose of each and all in the way he pleases, enable him to foresee events in his infinite knowledge and arrange the whole sequence of things in conformity with his plans, somewhat as an ingenious, skilful workman, by the aid of various colours, conceives of and arranges the life-like reproduction of a mosaic, a picture, or a piece of inlaid work. We understand all his forecasts of the future, how it was that Daniel foretold so exactly the greatness of Alexander and his conquests; how Isaiah called Cyrus by name many centuries before these mighty conquerors appeared to spread confusion and terror over the world; how God, in order to show forth his might before the nations and spread abroad the glory of his name, is said to have hardened Pharaoh's heart and roused his obstinate will; for all that was needed in order to bring to pass these various results was for God to call back into existence certain souls he knew to be naturally suited to his purpose. This is distinctly pointed out in the passage from the apostle St. Jude, which, if we accept the meaning that first offers itself to the mind, would seem positively to imply that certain souls had undergone a sentence of eternal reprobation: 'For there are certain men crept in unawares, who were before of old ordained to this condemnation, turning the grace of our God into lasciviousness....'"

"And so there falls away and disappears the greatest difficulty in the doctrine of grace, which consisted in explaining how it came about that God made some men pitiful and others hard-hearted, without there being in him either justice or acceptance of persons; showing pity, says St. Augustine, only by grace that was unmerited, and hardening hearts only by judgment that was always just; since evidently according to this theory it is not (as Origen has already said) apart from previous merit that some are formed for vessels of honour, and others for vessels of shame and wrath. That harsh sentence pronounced upon Judas by the Bishop of Hippon, which so grievously scandalised most of the Catholic theologians, although only the confirmation of the quotation from St. Jude, viz., that the wretched man had been predestined to shed the Saviour's blood, will seem to be a very just one in the sense that God causes that already lost soul to be born again, that demon, as Jesus Christ called him, for the very purpose of perpetrating the hateful crime.

"Consequently the most sublime mysteries of religion, the most wonderful facts regarding the destiny of the soul, find their natural explanation in a clear understanding of this doctrine of metempsychosis, however strange and extraordinary it may at first appear. What more striking proof can be asked for, what stronger and more convincing reason than such agreement, concerning matter wherein all positive proof will always, humanly speaking, be impossible? A doctrine which meets all the facts of the case so accurately, which explains, without difficulty, all the phenomena of our existence in this world, can, of necessity, be nothing else than true."

Jean Reynaud expresses himself in these terms in *Terre el Ciel*:

"How glorious the light that would be cast on the present order of things on earth by a knowledge of our former existences! And yet, not only is our memory helpless regarding the times that preceded birth, it is not even conscious of the whole of the intervening period, often playing us false in the course of a lifetime. It retains absolutely nothing of the period immediately preceding birth, and scarcely any trace of our education as children; we might even be altogether ignorant of the fact that we were children once, were there not around us witnesses of that time. On every hand we are wrapped in a veil of ignorance, as with a pall of darkness, we no more distinguish the light beyond the cradle than that beyond the tomb. So far as memory is concerned, it would seem that we might be compared with a rocket such as we sometimes see flashing through the sky in the night-time, leaving behind it a line of light, this light never shows anything more than a limited portion of the way. Of like nature is memory, a trail of light left behind on our journey; we die, and everything is dark around us; we are born again, and the light begins to appear, like a star through the mist; we live, and it develops and grows, suddenly disappears again and reappears once more; from one eclipse to another we continue our way, and this way, interrupted by periods of darkness, is a continuous one, whose elements, only apparently separated, are linked to each other by the closest of bonds; we always bear within ourselves the principle of what we shall be later on, we are always rising higher. Question us on our past, and, like the rocket, we reply that we are going forward, but that our path is illumined only in our immediate neighbourhood, and that the rest of the road is lost in the blackness of night; we no more know from where we came than we know our destination, but we do know that we came from below and are rising higher, and that is all that is necessary to interest us in ourselves and make us conscious of what we are. And who knows but what our soul, in the unknown secret of its essence, has power some day to throw light on its successive journeyings, like those streaks of flame to which we are comparing it? There are strong reasons for thinking that such is the case, since the entire restoration of memory appears, with good reason, to be one of the main conditions of our future happiness....

"In like manner the soul, passing from one abode to another, and leaving its first body for a new one, ever changing its appearance and its dwelling, guided by the Creator's beams, from transmigration to transmigration, from metamorphosis to metamorphosis, pursues the palingenesic course of its eternal destiny....

"... Let us, then, add the teachings of metempsychosis to those of the Gospel, and place Pythagoras by the side of Jesus...."

Andre Pezzani concludes in the following words his remarkable book on *The Plurality of the Soul's Lives*:

"Apart from the belief in previous lives, nothing can be explained, neither the coming of a new soul into this evil world, the often incurable bodily infirmities, the disproportionate division of wealth, nor the inequality in intelligence and morality. The justice of God lies behind the monstrous phantom of chance. We understand neither what man is, whence he comes, nor whither he goes; original sin does not account for the particular fate of individuals, as it is the same for all. Roughly speaking, it clears up no difficulties, but rather adds to them the most revolting injustice. Once accept the theory of pre-existence, and a glorious light is thrown on the dogma of sin, for it becomes the result of personal faults from which the guilty soul must be purified.

"Pre-existence, once admitted as regards the past, logically implies a succession of future existences for all souls that have not yet attained to the goal and that have imperfections and defilements from which to be cleansed. In order to enter *the circle of happiness* and leave *the circle of wanderings*, one must be pure.

"We have opposed error, and proclaimed truth, and we firmly believe that the dogmas of pre-existence and the plurality of lives are true."

Thomas Browne, in *Religio Medici*, section 6, hints at Reincarnation:

"Heresies perish not with their authors, but, like the river Arethusa, though they lose their currents in one place, they rise up again in another ... revolution of time will restore it, when it will flourish till it be condemned again. For as though there were a Metempsychosis, and the soul of one man passed into another, opinions do find, after certain Revolutions, men and minds like those that first begat them.... Each man is not only himself, there hath been many Diogenes and as many Timons, though but few of that name; men are lived over again, the world is now as it was in ages past; there was none then but there hath been someone since that parallels him, and is, as it were, his revived self."

Lessing, in *The Divine Education of the Human Race*, vigorously opposes a Lutheran divine who rejects reincarnation:

"The very same way by which the race reaches its perfection must every individual man—one sooner, another later—have travelled over. Have travelled over in one and the same life? Can he have been in one and the self-same life a sensual Jew and a spiritual Christian?

"Surely not that! But why should not every individual man have existed more than once in this world?

"Is this hypothesis so laughable merely because it is the oldest? Because the human understanding, before the sophistries of the schools had disciplined and debilitated it, lighted upon it at once? Why may not even I have already performed those steps of my perfecting which bring to men only temporal punishments and rewards? And once more, why not another time all those steps, to perform which the views of Eternal Rewards so powerfully assist us? Why should I not come back as often as I am capable of acquiring fresh knowledge, fresh expertness? Do I bring away so much from once that there is nothing to repay the trouble of coming back?

"Is this a reason against it? Or because I forget that I have been here already? Happy is it for me that I do forget. The recollection of my former condition would permit me to make only a bad use of the present. And that which even I must forget *now*, is that necessarily forgotten for ever?"

Schlosser gives expression to similar thoughts in a fine work of his: *Ueber die Seelenwanderung*.

Lichtemberg says in his *Seibstcharacteristik*:

"I cannot get rid of the thought that I died before I was born, and that by this death I was led to this rebirth. I feel so many things that, were I to write them down, the world would regard me as a madman. Consequently, I prefer to hold my peace."

Charles Bonnet is the author of a splendid work, full of noble and lofty thoughts, on this subject. It is entitled *Philosophic Palingenesis*.

Emmanuel Kant believes that our souls start imperfect from the sun, and travel through planetary stages farther and farther away to a paradise in the coldest and remotest star in our system. (*General History of Nature*.)

In *The Destiny of Man*, J. G. Fichte says:

"These two systems, the purely spiritual and the sensuous— which last may consist of an immeasurable series of particular lives—exist in me from the moment when my active reason is developed and pursue their parallel course....

"All death in nature is birth.... There is no death-bringing principle in nature, for nature is only life throughout.... Even because Nature puts me to death, she must quicken me anew...."

Herder, in his *Dialogues on Metempsychosis*, deals with this subject more fully:

"Do you not know great and rare men who cannot have been what they are in a single human existence; who must have often existed before in order to have attained that purity of feeling, that instinctive impulse for all that is true, beautiful, and good?... Have you never had remembrances of a former state?... Pythagoras, Iarchas, Apollonius, and others remembered distinctly what and how many times they had been in the world before. If we are blind or can see but two steps before our noses, ought we, therefore, to deny that others may see a hundred or a thousand degrees farther, even to the bottom of time ...?"

"He who has not become ripe in one form of humanity is put into the experience again, and, some time or other, must be perfected."

"I am not ashamed of my half-brothers the brutes; on the contrary, so far as I am concerned, I am a great advocate of metempsychosis. I believe for a certainty that they will ascend to a higher grade of being, and am unable to understand how anyone can object to this hypothesis, which seems to have the analogy of the whole creation in its favour."

Sir Walter Scott had such vivid memories of his past lives

that they compelled a belief in pre-existence. Instances of this belief may be found in *The Life of Scott*, by Lockhart (vol. 7, p. 114, first edition).

According to Schlegel:

"Nature is nothing less than the ladder of resurrection, which, step by step, leads upward, or rather is carried from the abyss of eternal death up to the apex of life." (*AEsthetic and Miscellaneous Works*; and, *The Philosophy of History*.)

Shelley held a firm belief in Reincarnation:

"It is not the less certain, notwithstanding the cunning attempts to conceal the truth, that all knowledge is reminiscence. The doctrine is far more ancient than the times of Plato," (Dowden's *Life of Shelley*, vol. 1, p. 82.)

Schopenhauer adopted the idea of Reincarnation which he had found in the *Upanishads*; regarding this portion of his teaching, his contemporaries and followers set up a kind of conspiracy of silence. In *Parerga and Paralipomena*, vol. 2, chap. 15, *Essay on Religions*, he says:

"I have said that the combination of the *Old Testament* with the *New* gives rise to absurdities. As an example, I may cite the Christian doctrine of Predestination and Grace as formulated by Augustine and adopted from him by Luther, according to which one man is endowed with grace and another is not. Grace thus comes to be a privilege received at birth and brought ready into the world.... What is obnoxious and absurd in this doctrine may be traced to the idea contained in the *Old Testament*, that man is the creation of an external will which called him into existence out of nothing. It is quite true that genuine moral excellence is really innate; but the meaning of the Christian doctrine is expressed in another and more rational way by the theory of Metempsychosis, common to Brahmans and Buddhists. According to this theory, the qualities which distinguish one man from another are received at birth, *i.e.*, are brought from another world and a former life; these qualities are not an external gift of grace, but are the fruits of the acts committed in that other world....

"What is absurd and revolting in this dogma is, in the main, as I said, the simple outcome of Jewish theism with its 'creation out of nothing,' and the really foolish and paradoxical denial of the doctrine of metempsychosis which is involved in that idea, a doctrine which is natural to a certain extent, self-evident, and, with the exception of the Jews, accepted by nearly the whole human race at all times.... Were an Asiatic to ask me for a definition of Europe, I should be forced to answer him: It is that part of the world which is haunted by the incredible delusion that man was created out of nothing, and that his present birth is his first entrance into life."

In *The World as Will and Idea*, he also says:

"What sleep is for the individual, death is for the Will (character)."

"It flings off memory and individuality, and this is Lethe; and through this sleep of death it reappears refreshed and fitted out with another intellect, as a new being."

In *Parerga and Paralipomena*, vol. 2, chap. 10, he adds:

"Did we clearly understand the real nature of our inmost being, we should see how absurd it is to desire that individuality should exist eternally. This wish implies that we confuse real Being with one of its innumerable manifestations. The individuality disappears at death, but we lose nothing thereby, for it is only the manifestation of quite a different Being—a Being ignorant of time, and, conesquently, knowing neither life nor death. The loss of intellect is the Lethe, but for which the Will would remember the various manifestations it has caused. When we die, we throw off our individuality, like a worn-out garment, and rejoice because we are about to receive a new and a better one."

Edgar Allen Poe, speaking of the dim memories of bygone lives, says:

"We walk about, amid the destinies of our world-existence, encompassed by divine but ever present Memories of a Destiny more vast—very distant in the bygone time and infinitely awful."

"We live out a Youth peculiarly haunted by such dreams, yet never mistaking them for dreams. As Memories we *know* them. During our *Youth* the distinction is too clear to deceive us even for a moment.

"But now comes the period at which a conventional World-Reason awakens us from the truth of our dream ... a misshapen day or a misfortune that could not be traced back to our own doings in this or in another life...." (*Eureka.*)

Georges Sand, in *Consuelo*, sets forth the logic of Reincarnation; and G. Flammarion expounds this doctrine in most of his works: *Uranie*; *Les Mondes Imaginaires et les Mondes Reels*; *La Pluralite des Mondes Habites*, etc.

Professor William Knight wrote in the *Fortnightly Review* for September, 1878:

"It seems surprising that in the discussions of contemporary philosophy on the origin and destiny of the soul there has been no explicit revival of the doctrines of Pre-existence and Metempsychosis.... They offer quite a remarkable solution of the mystery of Creation, Translation, and Extinction....

"Stripped of all extravagances and expressed in the modest terms of probability, the theory has immense speculative interest and great ethical value. It is much to have the puzzle of the origin of evil thrown back for an indefinite number of cycles of lives and to have a workable explanation of Nemesis...."

Professor W. A. Butler, in his *Lectures on the History of Ancient Philosophy*, says:

"There is internally no greater improbability that the present may be the result of a former state now almost wholly forgotten than that the present should be followed by a future form of existence in which, perhaps, or in some departments of which, the oblivion may be as complete."

The Rev. William R. Alger, a Unitarian minister, adds:

"Our present lack of recollection of past lives is no disproof of their actuality.... The most striking fact about the doctrine of the repeated incarnations of the soul ... is the constant reappearance of that faith in all parts of the world and its permanent hold on certain great nations....

"The advocates of the resurrection should not confine their attention to the repellent or ludicrous aspects of metempsychosis, ... but do justice to its claim and charm." (*A Critical History of the Doctrine of a Future Life.*)

Professor Francis Bowen, of Harvard University, writes in the *Princetown Review* for May, 1881, when dealing with the subject of *Christian Metempsychosis*:

"Our life upon earth is rightly held to be a discipline and a preparation for a higher and eternal life hereafter. But if limited to the duration of a single mortal body, it is so brief as to seem hardly sufficient for so great a purpose.... Why may not the probation of the soul be continued or repeated through a long series of successive generations, the same personality animating, one after another, an indefinite number of tenements of flesh, and carrying forward into each the training it has received, the character it has formed, the temper and dispositions it has indulged, in the stage of existence immediately preceding?...

"Every human being thus dwells successively in many bodies, even during one short life.[232] If every birth were an act of absolute creation, the introduction to life of an entirely new creature, we might reasonably ask why different souls are so variously constituted at the outset.... One child seems a perverse goblin, while another has the early promise of a Cowley or a Pascal.... The birthplace of one is in Central Africa, and of another in the heart of civilised and Christian Europe. Where lingers eternal justice then? How can such frightful inequalities be made to appear consistent with the infinite wisdom and goodness of God?...

"If metempsychosis is included in the scheme of the divine government of the world, this difficulty disappears altogether. Considered from this point of view, everyone is born into the state which he has fairly earned by his own previous history.... We submit with enforced resignation to the stern decree; ... that the iniquities of the fathers shall be visited upon the children even to the third and fourth generation. But no one can complain of the dispositions and endowments which he has inherited, so to speak, from himself, that is, from his former self in a previous stage of existence.

"And it matters not, so far as the justice of the sentence is concerned, whether the former self from whom we receive this heritage bore the same name with our present self, or bore a different name...."

Professor F. H. Hedge, in *Ways of the Spirit, and other Essays*, p. 359, maintains that:

"Whatever had a beginning in time, it should seem, must end in time. The eternal destination which faith ascribes to the soul presupposes an eternal origin.... An obvious objection, and one often urged against this hypothesis, is the absence of any recollection of a previous life.... The new organisation with its new entries must necessarily efface the record of the old. For memory depends on continuity of association. When the thread of that continuity is broken, the knowledge of the past is gone....

"And a happy thing, if the soul pre-existed, it is for us that we remember nothing of its former life.... Of all the theories respecting the origin of the soul this seems to me the most plausible, and therefore the one most likely to throw light on the question of a life to come."

The Spiritualists of Europe—those belonging to the school of Allan Kardec, at all events—place reincarnation in the very forefront of their teaching. We may add that those of America do not acknowledge that the soul has more than one existence on earth, driven, however, by the logic of things, which insists on progress, they state that there are a series of lives passed in subtler bodies on invisible planets and worlds.

All true philosophers have been attracted by the mystery of palingenesis, and have found that its acceptance has thrown a flood of light on the questions that perplexed them.

In Asia there are 400 millions of believers in reincarnation, including the Chinese, Tartars, Thibetans, Hindus, Siamese, Mongolians, Burmese, Cambodians, Koreans, and the people of Japan.

Tradition has handed down this teaching even to the most savage tribes. In Madagascar, when a man is on the point of death, a hole is made in the roof of his straw hut, through which his soul may pass out and enter the body of a woman in labour. This may be looked upon as a stupid superstition, still it is one which, in spite of its degenerate form, sets forth the doctrine of the return of souls back to evolution through earthly experiences. The Sontals, Somalis, and Zulus, the Dyaks of Borneo and Sumatra, and the Powhatans of Mexico have similar traditions. In Central Africa, slaves who are hunchbacked or maimed forestall the hour of death by voluntary self-immolation, in the hope of being reborn in the bodies of men who will be free and perfectly formed.

To sum up: all tradition, whether popular, philosophical, or religious, is instinct with the teaching of Rebirth.

OBJECTION

Reincarnation and Forgetfulness of the Past.

Sceptics are ever bringing forward against reincarnation the absence of all memory of past lives, convinced that there can be no answer to this argument.

They do not reflect that human ignorance is a bottomless abyss, whilst the possibilities of Life are endless. The schools of the future will smile at the claims made by those of the present, just as the latter doubtless regard with pitying indulgence that school which, only a few years ago, in the person of one of its most famous members, Dr. Bouillaud, mercilessly condemned the exponent of Edison's invention, because the *savant*, listening to a phonograph for the first time, could not believe that it was anything else than ventriloquism! Instances of this kind are sufficiently numerous and recent not to be forgotten, in spite of the shortness of human memory.

In the present instance, there are many men of science who have not yet been made sufficiently wise by experience to see that the very mystery of memory itself might furnish an explanation of that general absence of all power of recollection, which now seems to them altogether incompatible with the doctrine of Rebirth.

So as not to appear to be running away from this objection, by dealing with it only on the surface, we will endeavour to develop the question somewhat, for we shall have to set forth to readers unacquainted with theosophical teachings—which alone, up to the present, have thrown light on these difficult subjects—certain doctrines which will be well understood by none but theosophists, since they are incapable of proof by a simple statement thereof, but form part, of a long chain of teachings. We will offer them simply as theories—though they are facts to us—theories that contain many an error, it may be, and are imperfectly stated, though capable of widening the horizon of thought and shedding a brilliant light upon many an obscure question. Earnest seekers after truth, it is hoped, will not be disheartened by the difficulties of the subject, but will endeavour to grasp the meaning of the following pages, by reading them over again, if need be.

First, a few words must be said on memory in general, next we will give a rapid sketch of what constitutes memory in atoms and molecules, in the varied forms of the many

Th. Pascal

kingdoms of nature and in human forms; finally, we will speak of cosmic Memory, that veritable *Judgment Book* which takes account of all the vibrations of the Universe.

Amongst beings capable of memory, a distinction must be made between those which have not reached the stage of self-consciousness, and those which have done so, for memory, properly so-called, takes for granted an "I." That which has not an "I" can only have a memory of which it is not conscious[233]; the atom, for instance, of whose memory we shall speak later on; that which has only a rudimentary "I" possesses only a rudimentary memory from the point of view of its bearing on the individual—such is that possessed by the souls of the lower kingdoms, that which constitutes instinct; to the perfect "I" alone belongs an individual memory—the human memory, and that of beings who have attained to the superhuman stage. This memory may be defined as the faculty possessed by an individualised "centre of consciousness" voluntarily to reproduce the vibrations it has received or generated.

A "centre of consciousness" is a form that serves, for the time being, as the instrument of an individualised ray of that indefinable principle called the soul. But for the presence of this individual soul in a form, this latter would remain inactive as a centre of consciousness—although active in its constituent parts[234]—and could it not then, consciously, either generate or receive vibrations on the plane from which the soul is momentarily absent—it could only transmit them; for instance, when a man is in a brown study, he is not conscious in his brain, of what is taking place on the physical plane.[235]

The vehicles of consciousness are often numerous in a being, and the more numerous in proportion to the degree this latter has attained in the scale of evolution. The present day man possesses four bodies: the visible, the astral, the mental, and the causal. They are not all equally developed, and therefore not equally conscious, for the clearness and intensity of consciousness depend on the decree of perfection of its vehicles, just as the beauty of electric light depends on the perfection of the apparatus producing it.

The Ego—the man—is the consciousness that is called forth by the soul in the causal body. This consciousness varies in power with the development of the body that gives birth to it. At first it is dim and uncertain,[236] and acquires some degree of intensity only when it receives, through the mental and astral vehicles, the simple and intense vibrations of the physical body.[237] In savage races, for instance, man possesses a definite consciousness only in his waking condition; as soon as the soul is attached to the astral body, externalised by sleep, it experiences only a dim consciousness in this undeveloped vehicle. In advanced races, the astral body, being far more developed, brings about distinct consciousness during sleep. As man evolves, consciousness begins to function in the mental and the astral bodies, without the assistance of the vibrations of the lower vehicles, and when all the grades[238] of matter which compose the human constitution are thus vitalised, man has become perfect; he knows the Universe because he feels it within himself—he echoes it, so to speak, and possesses all its powers.[239]

In ordinary man, the memory of events that have taken place in his waking state can be brought back by that special effort of will which sets in motion the cerebral molecules that have previously been put into vibration by these events.

Sometimes the will, of itself, is powerless to recall this vibration, either because the brain is tired or in some unfavourable condition or other; it is then aided by bringing

Th. Pascal

its automatism into play, by endeavouring, for instance, to call back one constituent element of the fact desired, a place, sound, scent, person, &c, and often in this way is brought about the vibration of the molecules that constituted the rest of the circuit, and the fact sought for presents itself; association of ideas is a phenomenon based on this mechanical process.

A third method—a far more difficult one—is also used; the bringing of every mental effort, to a standstill. The suppression of thought, when sufficiently complete, brings the brain into a state of calm, allows of the soul concentrating on the astral body whose memory is keen and only slightly subject to obstruction, and then it often happens that the vibration of the astral memory repercusses on to the physical apparatus which suddenly remembers the thing desired.

On the death of the physical, the soul acts in the astral body; there it retains a complete memory of life on earth, but the vibrations of the physical plane no longer reach it,[240] these memories soon cease to occupy its attention, and it gives itself up wholly to the impressions received from the new world into which it has entered. In this first stage of the after-life, then, there is a kind of darkening of the memory of the past earth life—darkening, not oblivion.

When the purgatorial life is at an end and the astral body disintegrates in its turn, the soul functions in the mental body, in the mental world.[241] On this new plane, the memory of the worlds left behind continues, though far less clearly than the memory of the physical existed in the astral world; this is owing to the fact that, in ordinary man, the mental body is not sufficiently developed to constitute a complete vehicle of consciousness, capable of registering all the vibrations that come to it; everything in the past that has been *purely* the work of the astral or the physical plane then disappears from his memory; there remain only memories that have been caused either by the mental qualities or qualities superior to these, all the highest elements concerned with affection, intelligence, or art. The mental world, generally speaking, is seen only to a small extent or not at all, because of the incomplete development of the mental body. Besides, recollections assume a new character[242]; every thought takes a concrete form—that of a friend, for instance, appears as the friend himself, speaking and thinking, more vivid than on the earth plane[243]; everything is dramatised in marvellous fashion, and life is intense throughout the realms of paradise.

The mental body, after exhausting the forces that make it up, also dies, and the soul is "centred" in the only vehicle it has left, the causal body, a body that is immortal, one may say, up to a certain point, since the soul retains it until the time comes when it can function in a still higher and more lasting vehicle,[244] and this happens only after millions of years.[245] Here, another diminution of memory takes place, because the soul loses a large portion of its consciousness when it comes into contact with none but the vibrations of this body, which is even more incompletely developed than the former ones, though holding within itself all the germs of these latter. The Ego then remains apparently sunk in sleep for a varying period, though never for very long; then the germs in the causal body become active, build up a new series of bodies in succession—the mental, the astral, and finally the physical—and the soul returns once more to incarnation.

It will now be understood how it comes about that a soul of average development—on entering a new cycle, with the memory of the last cycle considerably obliterated by the loss of the physical, astral, and mental bodies, sheathed in new bodies on these planes, bodies that have nothing in common with the life of the past—is unable to impress its dim memories on to the brain; but it will also be seen that, with the progress of evolution, the soul acquires ever clearer consciousness in the causal body, in which it finally preserves the memory of the various life-cycles. Since, at this stage, it has become capable of projecting its vibrations, voluntarily, through the lower bodies, it is able to transmit this memory first to the mental body, then to the astral, and lastly to the physical body; when this is possible, man, in waking consciousness, remembers his former lives.

This transmission requires a purificatory process in the vehicles and a special training of the will. The matter of all the bodies—that of the brain in particular—must be refined, its constituent elements must be subtler, and its atoms must be fully awakened to activity[246]; whereupon the cerebral cell becomes capable of responding to the thought of the Ego, *i.e.*, of vibrating in harmony with the higher matter.

The second condition of the brain's receptivity is that this organ be brought into a state of complete rest. So long as the waking consciousness is active, the brain vibrates power-fully, and if, at this time, the soul sends the brain its thought, this latter can no more make an impression on the existing cerebral activity than a faint note could be heard amid the clash of an orchestra. Consequently, man, by the training of his will, must have acquired the power to stop the thinking activity in the waking state, and to "centre" his attention on the causal body, the only vehicle in which he can know the facts of his past incarnations; this done he is able, at will, to project on to his brain the scenes of his former lives and to imprint them thereon with greater distinctness, in proportion to his development and training.

In order to avoid continued explanations, we will deal with

another side of the question, however incomprehensible it be to such as have not studied theosophy.

A vehicle of consciousness is both a registering apparatus[247] and a conductor of vibrations.[248] The kinds of matter of which forms are made up are perfectly graduated; the finest atom of the physical body is built up of the densest atoms of the astral plane, the finest atom of the astral body is made of the densest atoms of the mental plane, and so on. Each atom is linked to the one that precedes and to the one that follows it in that immense chain which stretches from the densest to the subtlest plane of the Cosmos. Every vibration follows this path, passes in all directions—in the seven[249] dimensions of space-and terminates in the very Centre of consciousness, the Logos, God incarnate in the world.

It is then comprehensible, even logical, that God should be both conscious, on his receptive side, of everything that takes place in the world (*omniscient*), and should produce, on his active side, all the forces of the world (*omnipotent*). It is likewise admissible that the human soul, when fully developed, should find in the causal body the memory of the facts that have echoed therein, from the time when it could function consciously in it. But, it will be asked, how could it find, in the causal body, memories of existences it has not been able to register individually, of which it has not been conscious, those, for instance, that form the early stages of its evolution at a time when it was conscious only in the lower vehicles?

Memory possesses many store-houses. The vibrations of which it is composed affect the whole Universe, there is not a single local shock that is not felt throughout all the worlds. The eternal registering of things takes place in the great centre of consciousness, God, or rather, it exists in him, for to him there is neither future nor past, only one eternal present; evolution is unceasingly accomplished[250]; but if we look upon ourselves as finite beings, living in the illusion of time and space, we find that vibrating matter preserves for a longer or a shorter period the movement imparted to it. The denser the substance, which forms the medium in which vibration takes place, the feebler the vibration; that is why it speedily ceases on the physical plane; it continues long, however, in the higher conditions of matter, and it is there we must look for it,[251] if we would recall certain events at which we have not been present. When anything exciting, a murder, a battle, for instance, has happened anywhere, the subtler atoms of the surrounding objects receive a powerful shock and continue to vibrate for centuries. Those who have developed their inner senses can thus witness the scene which is continually repeating itself, or rather, is happening all the time.[252] Thus, psychometrists,[253] in presence of a portion of a fossil, are enabled to bring back scenes that this fragment has witnessed millions of years ago.[254]

In these cases, the memory of the facts is connected with that of the atoms which register it; this memory can only be recalled by coming into contact with these atoms.[255]

There is also another memory, midway between the unconscious memory of atoms and the conscious memory of the human soul; that of the forms of the various sub-human kingdoms. It is only slightly conscious, for it is not individualised; all the same, it is precise in its nature. It dwells in the vital essence of the form, an essence taken from a collective "block" which supplies a portion of its substance to the individuals of the same species; this incarnate portion of essence, when the form disintegrates at death, returns to the parent "block," to which it communicates the result of its experiences, and when the latter sends out a portion of itself, into a new form, this tentacle, which is, so to speak, the soul of the form, is in possession of the whole of the experiences of the "block."[256] This explains how it is that the individual members of certain hostile species know one another from birth—the chicken, for instance, which, immediately it has left the egg, trembles before the hawk hovering above in the air; such is also the reason why a duckling plunges into water as soon as it comes to a pond, and the same instinct impels a bird to leave its nest and trust itself to the air when fully fledged.

In these collective souls, belonging to the mineral, vegetable, and animal kingdoms, there can be recovered the past to which they bore witness, when the atoms of their bodies have been dispersed and entered into new combinations.

When the elemental Essence[257] has definitely split up, and the "blocks" have become separate, individualised, human fragments,[258] each of these fragments is a causal body, a definite, immortal *centre* in the total Centre. Consequently there are in man three kinds of memory: atomic memory, that of the atoms of his bodies; instinctive memory of the special elemental essences which are the collective souls of his various vehicles; and finally, the individual memory of the centre,[259] which is one with the total Centre from which it comes.

This element of unity, this human "I" in the divine "I," when sufficiently developed, is able to evoke the memory of all the events in which it has participated in the causal body, and also the memory of those it has witnessed as a collective soul (elemental "block") in bygone ages when active in various mineral, vegetable, and animal species. As a centre in the great Centre, it can also call forth the memory of everything in the Universe that its consciousness can grasp.[260] And when, in this long pilgrimage, it has developed to the farthest limits of the Universe it knows all that has been, is now, and is to be in this Universe, consequently it knows both what it has and what it has not participated in, for everything in the Universe has then become part of itself.

Thus it is seen that the memory of the past is everywhere registered, and that the difficulty a man has in bringing it back is caused by nothing more than his imperfect development. Once he has entered the "Strait Gate,"[261] and his consciousness is awake on the first plane of Unity,[262] he becomes able to read the Great Book of Nature, in which all vibrations are kept in potentiality; he can revive them by an effort of will, similar to that he makes in a waking state, when he wishes to bring back past impressions to his brain. The difference lies in the fact that, in the latter case, being in the physical body, he calls up the memory retained in the astral body; whilst in the former case, being in the causal body, he brings memory within the influence of the buddhic body, or even at times of higher bodies still. The more the Being grows, and becomes able to fix his consciousness on the higher planes, the wider extends his sphere of influence, approaching that of divine Consciousness.

It is ignorance that brings forward this objection regarding loss of memory, ignorance of life and of death, ignorance of the phenomena that follow the last breath of a dying man, as well as of those preceding the first faint cry of a new-born child. Sceptics, however, might have shown a little more indulgence, for, as they are well aware, ordinary memory *is* even now so unreliable that a man has great difficulty in recalling the whole of the thoughts that have entered his brain during the last few minutes; he has forgotten the details of the various events of the week; the facts of the past year have mostly vanished from his mind, and when he comes to the end of the journey, mere fragments of the story of his life are all that is left. For all that, he has all the time retained the notion of the identity of his "I"; he has the same body, the same senses, and the same brain; his environment is the same; everything is there to bring about association of ideas, to awaken memory. On the other hand, centuries have elapsed before Rebirth takes place; the human being has undergone the most radical changes and modifications; everything in him that was perishable has disappeared, and is preserved only in a germinal state. The visible bodily sheath has had its atoms scattered to the four elements; the etheric body[263] has become separated from the physical molecules whose vital support it formed; the body of passions and desires (*astral body*) has lived for a few years in what Catholics call *Purgatory*, Greeks, *Hades*, and Hindus, *Kamaloka*; after which, only germs have been left behind; then the intelligence (*mental body*) has been dispersed in turn and endures only in a germinal state. Almost everything that made up the man of bygone times has disappeared, and is now concentrated in a complex germ hidden away in the causal body and destined to develop a new personality later on,[264] heir to the former one, though it will not be capable of remembering events in which it took no part.

This is the explanation of the myth of Lethe.

The soul, in the causal body, drinks of the river of Life, and from its sleep-giving draught forms the sheaths of the new incarnation, the new bodies that altogether blot out the memory of the past; it is, in very truth, a new-born babe who appears on earth.

The Root-Being,[265] however, survives the successive wrecks of fleeting personalities, remaining in the new man as a guide, as the "Voice of Conscience." He is the Watcher who strings, as on a thread, the numberless pearls (*personalities*) which form the inevitable cycle of human evolution, and is able, when fully developed, to summon up

Th. Pascal

the distant panorama of past lives. For him, nothing is lost.

The pioneers of the race have obtained direct proof of successive incarnations, but apart from these rare and special instances, ordinary individuals frequently have reminiscences and distinct memories which are not investigated, either because they are fragmentary in their nature or are related by children. In India, where the natives believe in Reincarnation, such cases are regarded without astonishment, and efforts are made to prove their truth by serious investigation, whenever possible. And such proof is often possible. When a child dies in infancy, before he is able to use his body intelligently and of his own free will—before being able to generate karma the higher sheaths (*the astral and mental bodies*) are not separated into their component parts. Return to earth quickly takes place, the memory of the past life exists in the astral body—which has not changed— and, more especially during the first few years of life, can be impressed on the new brain with tolerable ease, if this latter is at all delicately constituted. Then if reincarnation takes place in the same country and in the neighbourhood of the past incarnation, it can be proved to be true. Such instances do exist; the reason they are not mentioned here is that they would add nothing to the general proofs on which stress has been laid in this work. These proofs form part of universal Law; they cannot be separated therefrom.

FOOTNOTES:

[Footnote 81: The fifth, or Aryan race, in theosophic nomenclature; the fourth was that of Atlantis; the third lived on the great southern continent, Lemuria; the two preceding ones were, so to speak, only the embryologic preparation for the following races.]

[Footnote 82: The "life-atoms," infinitesimal particles which by aggregation form the human body. Certain of these atoms are preserved, on the death of the body, as germs which will facilitate the reconstruction of the physical body at the next rebirth.]

[Footnote 83: The divine Essence which animates animals, and so, in another sense the astral bodies of men and animals, bodies whose particles *transmigrate* as do the physical atoms.]

[Footnote 84: H. P. Blavatsky, *Secret Doctrine.*]

[Footnote 85: These words are relative; they express differences in the evolution of souls.]

[Footnote 86: The atmosphere of subtle physical elements radiating round the human body and acting in a defensive *role* by preventing the penetration of unhealthy elements from the immediate surroundings.]

[Footnote 87: The "material sin" of Manu.]

[Footnote 88: One, here means the "life atoms" of a man's body.]

[Footnote 89: The word is here used in a generic sense; in the present work, it would be more precise to replace it by the word Resurrection.]

[Footnote 90: This "triad" comprises the visible matter of the body, the etheric substance, and the life (Prana) which the human ether absorbs and specialises for the vitalising of the body. See *Man and his Bodies*, by A. Besant.]

[Footnote 91: H. P. Blavatsky, *The Theosophist*, Vol. 4, pages 287, 288.]

[Footnote 92: The finer elements invisible to physical eye. Their function is sensation, and by their association with the human mental body incarnated in them, they give birth to the emotions and passions, in a word, to the animal in man.]

[Footnote 93: The *Umbra* of the Latin races.]

[Footnote 94: The *Kama Rupa* of the Hindus.]

[Footnote 95: The purgatory of Christians, the astral plane of theosophists, and the *Kamaloka* of Hindus.]

[Footnote 96: By the *fire* of purgatory, says the Catholic metaphor.]

[Footnote 97: See A. Besant's masterly work on *Reincarnation.*]

[Footnote 98: Dharma is a wide word, primarily meaning the essential nature of a thing; hence the laws of its being, its duty; and it includes religious rites, appropriate to those laws. This definition, as also the extracts quoted, are taken from A. Besant's translation of the *Bhagavad Gita.*]

[Footnote 99: Human souls, not all of them, but only the pious ones, are daimonic and divine. Once separated from the body, and after the struggle to acquire piety, which consists in knowing God and injuring none, such a soul becomes all intelligence. The impious soul, however, remains in its own essence and punishes itself by seeking a human body to enter into, for no other body can receive a human soul, it cannot enter the body of an animal devoid of reason: divine law preserves the human soul from such infamy. Hermes Trismegistus, Book I, *Lacle*: Hermes to his son Tat.]

[Footnote 100: Bodies.]

[Footnote 101: The physical body with its etheric "double," and life (*Prana*).]

[Footnote 102: The kamic body.]

[Footnote 103: The causal body.]

[Footnote 104: *History*. Book 2, chap. 123.]

[Footnote 105: The causal body.]

[Footnote 106: The buddhic body, which, in ordinary man, is only in an embryonic stage.]

[Footnote 107: Generally called *Prana*, in man. *Jiva* is the solar life which, on being transmuted by the physical body, becomes *Prana*, the human physical life. Both *Jiva* and *Prana* differ from each other in nature and in vibration.]

[Footnote 108: The mental body.]

[Footnote 109: The causal body. In annihilation—what has been called the loss of the soul—the kamic principle (astral body) in the course of a rather long succession of lives, does not allow the mental body to become separated from it in purgatory; it keeps it imprisoned up to the time of its disintegration; the causal body reaps nothing from the incarnations, at each re-birth it loses the forces it is putting forth in order to form the new mental body. It gradually atrophies until the time comes when it is no longer fit to make use of the ordinary bodies of the race to which it belongs. Then it remains at rest, whilst the mental body gradually disintegrates; afterwards it takes up once again its series of incarnations in the imperfectly evolved bodies of primitive races. This will be understood only by those who have studied theosophy.]

[Footnote 110: In this passage, H. P. Blavatsky alludes to the few etheric, astral, and mental atoms which, at each disincarnation, are incorporated in the causal body and form the nuclei of the future bodies corresponding to them.]

[Footnote 111: *History*. Vol. 2, book 2, chap. 123 (already quoted).]

[Footnote 112: Of the elements of the personality—of the astral body, in all probability.]

[Footnote 113: The Ego (soul) also lives in the air (the symbol of heaven) and on the earth (whose symbol is water, dense matter)—in heaven, after disincarnation; on earth, during incarnation.]

[Footnote 114: The soul is immortal and needs no food.]

[Footnote 115: Its name, Khopiroo, comes from the root Koproo, to become, to be born again (H. P. Blavatsky).

Hartley says: "At the centre of the solar disk appears the Scarabeus as the symbol of the soul re-uniting itself with the body. The Scarabeus is called by Pierret the synthesis of the Egyptian religion—type of resurrection—of self-existence—of self-engendering like the Gods. As Tori, or Chepi, the Sun is the Scarabeus, or self-engenderer, and the mystery of God."]

[Footnote 116: Also called kamic body, astral body, body of desire, etc.]

[Footnote 117: Reincarnation.]

[Footnote 118: Vol. 3, p. 124.]

[Footnote 119: The causal body illumined by the divine Essence, which theosophy names Atma-Buddhi.]

[Footnote 120: He calls him "the prince of lying fathers and dishonest writers." (*Egypt*, vol. 1, p. 200).]

[Footnote 121: Eusebius even confesses this himself: "I have set forth whatever is calculated to enhance the glory of our religion, and kept back everything likely to cast a stain upon it." (*Proeparatio Evangelica.* Book 12, chap. 31).]

[Footnote 122: *Namae-Sat Vakhshur-i-Mahabad*, also in the fourth "Journey" in chap. 4 of *Jam-i-Kaikhoshru* (see *The Theosophist*, p. 333, vol. 21).]

[Footnote 123: See *Bardic Triads*, by E. Williams. Translated from the original Welsh.]

[Footnote 124: "'Abred' is the circle of the migrations through which every animated being proceeds from death: man has passed through it." *Triad* 13.

"Transmigration is in 'Abred.'" *Triad* 14.

"There are three primitive calamities in 'Abred': the necessity of evolution (of rebirths), the absence of memory (of past incarnations) and death (followed by rebirth)." *Triad* 18 (the words in parentheses are our own).

"By reason of three things man is subjected to 'Abred' (or transmigration): by the absence of the effort to attain knowledge, by non-attachment to good, and by attachment to evil. As the result of these, he descends into 'Abred,' to the stage corresponding to his development, and begins his

Th. Pascal

transmigrations anew." *Triad* 25.

"The three foundations of science are: complete trans-migration through every state of being, the memory of the details of each transmigration, the power to pass again at will through any state, to acquire experience and judgment, (*a*) This comes to pass in the circle of Gwynvyd." *Triad* 36.

(*a*) The liberated being has power to call up the past, to tune his consciousness with that of every being, to feel everything that being feels, to be that being.]

[Footnote 125: In the poem *Cad-Godden*, quoted by Pezzani in *La Pluralite des Existences de l'Ame*, p. 93. Taliesin is a generic name indicating a function rather than the name of an individual.]

[Footnote 126: *Gallic War* (Book 2, chap. 6). Valerius Maximus relates that these nations lent one another money which was to be paid back in the other world, and that at Marseilles a sweet-tasted poison was given to anyone who, wishing to commit suicide, offered the judges satisfactory reasons for leaving his body.]

[Footnote 127: *The Mystery of the Ages*, by the Duchesse de Pomar.]

[Footnote 128: In *Theologia* or the *Seven Adyta.*]

[Footnote 129: The "Cycle of Necessity" extends from the time when the soul begins to evolve to the moment when it attains to liberation.]

[Footnote 130: *Life of Pythagoras*. Book 8, chap. 14.]

[Footnote 131: Ovid's *Metamorphoses*. Book 15.]

[Footnote 132: All that remained of the shield was the carved ivory ornamentation, the iron had been eaten away by rust.]

[Footnote 133: Philostratus, *Life of Apollonius of Tyana.*]

[Footnote 134: Philostratus, *Life of Apollonius of Tyana.*]

[Footnote 135: Marinas, *Vita Procli.*]

[Footnote 136: The Ego, the human soul properly so-called, what Egypt named the liberated intelligence which resumes its sheath of light, and again becomes a "daimon" (*Maspero*). In antiquity the name of daimon was given to the human soul or to higher intelligences.]

[Footnote 137: *Hades*; the Purgatory of Catholics; the *Kamaloka* of Hindus.]

[Footnote 138: Allusion to the struggle which separates the mental from the astral body in Purgatory.]

[Footnote 139: *Kamaloka*; Purgatory.]

[Footnote 140: The subterranean hell, the lowest world in Purgatory.]

[Footnote 141: Plato's *Laws*, Book 10.]

[Footnote 142: Plato's *Republic*, Book 10.]

[Footnote 143: They are in the causal body.]

[Footnote 144: *Phaedo.*]

[Footnote 145: These considerations are taken from the writings of H. P. Blavatsky, and are also confirmed by modern criticism of biblical texts.]

[Footnote 146: Maimonides. Quoted in *The Perfect Way*, by A. Kingsford and E. Maitland.]

[Footnote 147: *Galatians*, chap. 4, verses 24, 25.]

[Footnote 148: *Starli*, part 4, p. 5.]

[Footnote 149: *Deuteronomy*, chap. 24, verses 1 to 4.]

[Footnote 150: *Deuteronomy*, chap. 17, verse 17.]

[Footnote 151: *Exodus*, chap. 21, verses 2 to 11.]

[Footnote 152: *Exodus*, chap. 21, verses 23, 24, 25.]

[Footnote 153: *Genesis*, chap. 9, verses 5, 6; also *Leviticus*, chap. 7.]

[Footnote 154: *Exodus*, chapters 6, 12, 14, 22, 32,]

[Footnote 155: *Ecclesiastes*, chap. 3, verses 18, 19, 20, 22.]

[Footnote 156: The souls of a race in its maturity are of a more advanced type than those of its infancy or old age.]

[Footnote 157: The Kabala is the secret teaching of the Jews; in it lie hidden doctrines that are too profound to be taught in public.]

[Footnote 158: *Zohar*, 2, 99, quoted in Myer's *Qabbalah*, p. 198.]

[Footnote 159: Evolution develops the soul, enabling it to reach its goal: the divine state.]

[Footnote 160: The force of evolution comes from God and ceases only when the soul is fully developed, and has reached the "promised land" at the end of its pilgrimage: the divine state.]

[Footnote 161: Franck, *La Kabbale*, p. 244, etc.]

[Footnote 162: *The Hidden Wisdom of Christ*, 1864, vol. 1, p. 39.]

[Footnote 163: *De Bell. jud.* 2, 11.]

[Footnote 164: One of the lowest sub-planes of *Kamaloka* (Purgatory).]

[Footnote 165: The Christian Heaven (*Devachan* of theosophy).]

[Footnote 166: The earth, which is above when compared with Tartarus, but not so in relation to the Elysian Fields; versification imposes such strict limits on expression, that it must have the benefit of poetic licence.]

[Footnote 167: Freret, *Examen crit. des apologistes de la relig. chret.*, pages 12 and 13, Paris, 1823.]

[Footnote 168: Faustus.]

[Footnote 169: And yet the *Gospel of Saint John* denies this (chap. 1, v. 21). The contradictions in the gospels are so numerous that they alone have created thousands of infidels.]

[Footnote 170: Stolberg expresses himself as follows on this matter: "This question was evidently based on the opinion that the disciples of Jesus had formed, that this man, whose punishment dated from his very birth, had sinned in a previous life." (*Histoire de N. S. Jesus-Christ et de son siecle*, Book 3, chap. 43).]

[Footnote 171: *Revelation*, chap. 3, v. 12.]

[Footnote 172: *Revelation*, chap. 2, v. 28.]

[Footnote 173: *Revelation*, chap. 22, v. 16.]

[Footnote 174: *Revelation*, chap. 2, v. 17.]

[Footnote 175: H. P. Blavatsky.]

[Footnote 176: "Taken literally, the Book of the Creation gives us the most absurd and extravagant ideas of Divinity."]

[Footnote 177: First *Ennead*, chap. I.]

[Footnote 178: The Universe, which can exist only through *multiplicity*.]

[Footnote 179: Second *Ennead*, chap. 3.]

[Footnote 180: Second *Ennead*, chap. 8.]

[Footnote 181: Third *Ennead*, chap. 4.]

[Footnote 182: *Concerning Abstinence*; Book 2.]

[Footnote 183: *Egyptian Mysteries*, Book 4, chap. 4.]

[Footnote 184: Here, *reincarnation* is meant.]

[Footnote 185: This philosopher was surnamed *Peisithanatos* (the death-persuader).]

[Footnote 186: *Vie de Pythagore*, vol. I, p. 28.]

[Footnote 187: *Hist. de l'Ec. a'Alex.*, vol. I, p 588.]

[Footnote 188: In this work, he says:

"The winged tribe, that has feathers instead of hair, is formed of innocent but superficial human beings, pompous and frivolous in speech, who, in their simplicity, imagine that the sense of vision is the best judge of the existence of things. Those who take no interest whatever in philosophy become four-footed animals and wild beasts...."]

[Footnote 189: *Commentaries on the Golden Verses of Pythagoras.*]

[Footnote 190: Hermes, *Commentaries of Chalcidius on the Timaeus.*]

[Footnote 191: *Procli Diadochi in Platonis Timaeum Commentaria.*]

[Footnote 192: September, 1898, p. 3.]

[Footnote 193: The life of the animal to which it is bound.]

[Footnote 194: The instrument must be suited to the development of the artist; too highly developed a body would be bad for a man very low down in the scale of humanity. This will, in some measure, explain the paradoxical word here used; the *advantage* there may sometimes be in putting on a rudimentary body.]

[Footnote 195: G. R. S. Mead tells us that Justin believed in Reincarnation only whilst he was a Platonist; he opposed this teaching after his conversion to Christianity (See *Theosophical Review*, April, 1906).]

[Footnote 196: Does this obscure passage refer to the resurrection of the body?]

[Footnote 197: *Adversus Gentes.* "We die many times, and as often do we rise again from the dead."]

[Footnote 198: Hyeronim., *Epistola ad Demetr....*]

[Footnote 199: Book 2, quest. 6, No. 17.]

[Footnote 200: *Ephesians*, ch. 1, v. 4 ... he hath chosen us in him before the foundation of the world.]

[Footnote 201: *Instit. divin.*, 3, 18.]

[Footnote 202: *Confessions*, I, ch. 6.]

[Footnote 203: *On the Immortality of the Soul*, chap. 12.]

[Footnote 204: *Hist. de Manichee et du Manicheisme*, vol. 2, p. 492.]

[Footnote 205: *Stromata.*, vol. 3, p. 433. Edition des Benedictins.]

[Footnote 206: The words in parenthesis are by the author.]

[Footnote 207: *Cont. Cels.* Book 4, chap. 17.]

[Footnote 208: [Greek: ti akolouthei].]

[Footnote 209: *De Principiis*, Book 3, chap. 5.]

[Footnote 210: *Contra Celsum*, Book 1.]

[Footnote 211: *Contra Celsum*, Book 1, chap. 6.]

[Footnote 212: *De Principiis*, Book 3, chap. 5.]

[Footnote 213: *De Principiis*, Book 4, chap. 5.]

[Footnote 214: *Contra Celsum*, Book 7, chap. 32.]

[Footnote 215: E. Aroux. *Les Mysteres de la Chevalerie.*]

[Footnote 216: Quoted by I. Cooper Oakley in *Traces of a Hidden Tradition in Masonry and Mediaeval Mysticism*, a very interesting work on the sects which connect the early centuries with modern times.]

[Footnote 217: See *L'Islamisme et son Enseignement Esoterique*, by Ed. Bailly. *Publications theosophiques*, Paris, 1903.]

[Footnote 218: Chapter 18.]

[Footnote 219: Islam is now awaiting the coming of the Mahdi, its last prophet; prophecy says that he will be the reincarnation of Mohammed (*Borderland*, April, 1907).]

[Footnote 220: This is the reason Afghans still undertake pilgrimages to Mecca.]

[Footnote 221: Chap. 22, verses 5, 14, 15, 17, 18, 19, 20, 41. Quoted by Lady Caithness in *Old Truths in a New Light.*]

[Footnote 222: Chap. 23, verses 17, 26, 27, etc.]

[Footnote 223: By religion is here understood the devotional aspect and the scientific side of the teaching of Truth, *i.e.*, the science of the divine Soul.]

[Footnote 224: *Nirmanakayas* are beings who have become perfect, and who, instead of entering the Nirvana their efforts have won, renounce peace and bliss in order to help forward their human brothers in their evolution.]

[Footnote 225:

> O! genus attonitum gelidae formidine mortis,
> Quid Styga, quid tenebras, quid nomina vana timetis,
> Materiam vatum, falsique piacula mundi?
> Corpora sive rogus flamma, seu tabe vetustas
> Abstulerit, mala posse pati non ulla putetis
> Morte carent animae: semperque priore relicta
> Sede, novis domibus habitant vivuntque receptae
> . . . .
> Omnia mutantur, nihil interit ...]

[Footnote 226: *S. John's Gospel*, chap. 9, verse 2.]

[Footnote 227: The following passages are taken from three of C. Savy's works: *Comment. du Sermon sur la Montagne* (1818); *Pensees et Meditations* (1829); *Dieu et l'Homme en cette Vie et Audela* (1838).]

[Footnote 228: *De l'Humanite*, vol. 1., p. 233.]

[Footnote 229: *Theorie de l'Unite Universelle*, vol. 2, p. 304-348.]

[Footnote 230: *Vie Future au Point de Vue Socialiste*, and *Confession d'un Cure de Village.*]

[Footnote 231: *Destinees de l'Ame.*]

[Footnote 232: Alluding to the complete renewing of the material molecules of the body, every seven years.]

[Footnote 233: Whose consciousness, however (along with memory), is at the summit of the hierarchy which is its origin.]

[Footnote 234: Molecules and atoms have a particular consciousness of their own which does not cease to function when, on the departure of the individual soul, the body, as such, ceases to function.]

[Footnote 235: If sufficiently developed, however, he can be made conscious of this in a higher vehicle.]

[Footnote 236: When man has barely entered the human stage—in primitive man.]

[Footnote 237: Consciousness begins in the physical body, its simplest instrument.]

[Footnote 238: There are other vehicles above the causal body.]

[Footnote 239: All the powers of the Universe are in the divine germ, as the tree is in its seed.]

[Footnote 240: Because it no longer has a dense physical body. There are exceptions to this rule, but there is no necessity to mention them here.]

[Footnote 241: The Christian Heaven, the *Devachan* of Theosophy.]

[Footnote 242: This character has already appeared on the astral plane, though not in so striking a fashion.]

[Footnote 243: Unity exists on the plane of the Ego, and the latter sends his thought into the forms made out of his vehicles; this will be understood only by the few, but an explanation cannot be given at this point, without writing a volume on the whole of theosophy.]

[Footnote 244: We are still dealing with the ordinary man.]

[Footnote 245: When liberation is attained. This can be effected rapidly by those who *will* to attain it.]

[Footnote 246: Only four of the seven atomic *spirillae* are active in this our fourth planetary Round (one for each Round). They can be rapidly vitalised by the will.]

[Footnote 247: When the soul is "centred" in it.]

[Footnote 248: The vibrations, whether registered as they pass or not registered, continue their course through the substance of the Universe.]

[Footnote 249: Science even now recognises four of these dimensions.]

[Footnote 250: This is said in order to satisfy such as are of a metaphysical turn of mind, and frequently prone to criticism.]

[Footnote 251: When the inner senses are developed.]

[Footnote 252: A question will doubtless at once rise to the minds of many readers; how can the same atoms produce, at once and almost eternally, millions of different facts? We will reply briefly. Science has been able to conceive of an explanation of a fact apparently quite as absurd—the phenomenon of the balls of Russian platinum mentioned by

Zoellner (*Transcendental Physics*, ch. 9) which pass through hermetically sealed glass tubes, and that of the German copper coins dropping through the bottom of a sealed box on to a slate—by accepting a fourth dimension of space. Who would affirm that the dimensions of space are limited to four? Or that the science of the immediate future will not be brought face to face with facts, and find, in a fifth or sixth dimension of space, a possible explanation of the phenomenon here mentioned, one which initiated seers can test whenever they please, because it is a real fact?

Still, as these seers say, the coarsest atoms generally register only one image, others register fresh images, so that in many cases there is quite a superposition of images which must be carefully examined to avoid errors.]

[Footnote 253: A psychometrist is a person endowed with a very fine nervous system, capable of repeating the delicate vibrations which act upon the inmost atoms of a body. In this way, by placing himself in presence of an object that has been in contact with some individual, he can clearly describe the latter's physical, moral, and mental characteristics. Hitherto, Buchanan and Professor Denton have been the most remarkable psychometrists; the experiments related in their works have been made before witnesses and permit of no doubt whatever as to the reality of this strange faculty.]

[Footnote 254: Instances of this are numerous in Professor Denton's *The Soul of Things*.]

[Footnote 255: This memory is preserved in the first "life-wave."]

[Footnote 256: This is *instinct*, *i.e.*, a semi-conscious memory, located in the "life-wave" of the second Logos.]

[Footnote 257: The divine Essence incarnated in the matter of the lower planes of the Universe.]

[Footnote 258: When the "essence," after the destruction of the form to which it gives life, no more returns to the parent-block from which it came, it has become individualised, ready to enter into the *human kingdom.*]

[Footnote 259: The memory of the third life-wave, of the first Logos.]

[Footnote 260: Everything, for instance, that concerns the planes of the planetary system, on which it has finished its evolution.]

[Footnote 261: The passing of consciousness from the causal body to the nascent buddhic body.]

[Footnote 262: The buddhic plane (the one immediately above the mental) is one in which the forms are so subtle that they no longer *limit* the Life (*the Soul of the World*) animating them. This Life comes directly into contact with the Life which causes all forms to live; it then sees Unity: it sees itself everywhere and in everything, the joys and sorrows of forms other than its own are its joys and sorrows, for it is universal Life.]

[Footnote 263: This body is composed of physical matter, and therefore belongs to the physical plane. It has been given a special name, not only because it is made of ether, but because it can be separated from the physical body.]

[Footnote 264: The whole of the bodies: mental, astral, and physical.]

[Footnote 265: The Ego (soul) in the causal body.]

CONCLUSION

We have now come to the end of our study: a task to which we have certainly not been equal, so far is it beyond our powers. As, however, we have drawn inspiration from our predecessors, so have we also, in our turn, endeavoured to shed a few more rays of light on certain points of this important subject, and indicate fresh paths that may be followed by such as enter upon this line of investigation in the future.

It is our most ardent desire to see this fertile soil well tilled, for it will yield an abundant harvest. Mankind is dying in strife and despair; the torrent of human activity is every-where seething and foaming. Here ignorance buries its victims in a noisome den of slime and filth; there, the strong and ruthless, veritable vampires, batten on the labour and drain away the very life of the weak and helpless; farther away, science stumbles against the wall of the Unknown; philosophy takes up its stand on the cold barren glacier of intellectualism; religions are stifled and struggle for existence beneath the age-long accumulations of the "letter that killeth." More now than ever before do we need to find a reason for morality, a guide for science, an Ariadne's thread for philosophy, a torch to throw light on religion, and Love over all, for if mankind continues to devote the whole of its strength to the pursuit of material benefits, if its most glorious conquests become instruments to advance selfishness, if its progress merely increases physical wretchedness and makes moral decadence more terrible than before, if the head continues to silence the appeals of the heart, then divine Compassion will have no alternative but to destroy beneath the waters of another flood this cruel, implacable civilisation, which has transformed earth into an inferno.

Amongst the most pressing and urgent truths, the most fruitful teachings, the most illuminating doctrines, the most comforting promises, we have no hesitation in placing the Law of Rebirths in the very front. It is supported by ethics, by reason, and by science; it offers an explanation of the enigma of life, it alone solves almost all the problems that have harassed the mind of man throughout the ages; and so we hope that, in spite of its many imperfections, this work of ours will induce many a reader to say: *Reincarnation must be true, if could not be otherwise!*

THE END

Choose from Thousands of 1stWorldLibrary Classics By

A. M. Barnard
Ada Leverson
Adolphus William Ward
Aesop
Agatha Christie
Alexander Aaronsohn
Alexander Kielland
Alexandre Dumas
Alfred Gatty
Alfred Ollivant
Alice Duer Miller
Alice Turner Curtis
Alice Dunbar
Allen Chapman
Alleyne Ireland
Ambrose Bierce
Amelia E. Barr
Amory H. Bradford
Andrew Lang
Andrew McFarland Davis
Andy Adams
Angela Brazil
Anna Alice Chapin
Anna Sewell
Annie Besant
Annie Hamilton Donnell
Annie Payson Call
Annie Roe Carr
Annonaymous
Anton Chekhov
Archibald Lee Fletcher
Arnold Bennett
Arthur C. Benson
Arthur Conan Doyle
Arthur M. Winfield
Arthur Ransome
Arthur Schnitzler
Arthur Train
Atticus
B.H. Baden-Powell
B. M. Bower
B. C. Chatterjee
Baroness Emmuska Orczy
Baroness Orczy
Basil King
Bayard Taylor
Ben Macomber
Bertha Muzzy Bower
Bjornstjerne Bjornson

Booth Tarkington
Boyd Cable
Bram Stoker
C. Collodi
C. E. Orr
C. M. Ingleby
Carolyn Wells
Catherine Parr Traill
Charles A. Eastman
Charles Amory Beach
Charles Dickens
Charles Dudley Warner
Charles Farrar Browne
Charles Ives
Charles Kingsley
Charles Klein
Charles Hanson Towne
Charles Lathrop Pack
Charles Romyn Dake
Charles Whibley
Charles Willing Beale
Charlotte M. Braeme
Charlotte M. Yonge
Charlotte Perkins Stetson
Clair W. Hayes
Clarence Day Jr.
Clarence E. Mulford
Clemence Housman
Confucius
Coningsby Dawson
Cornelis DeWitt Wilcox
Cyril Burleigh
D. H. Lawrence
Daniel Defoe
David Garnett
Dinah Craik
Don Carlos Janes
Donald Keyhoe
Dorothy Kilner
Dougan Clark
Douglas Fairbanks
E. Nesbit
E. P. Roe
E. Phillips Oppenheim
E. S. Brooks
Earl Barnes
Edgar Rice Burroughs
Edith Van Dyne
Edith Wharton

Edward Everett Hale
Edward J. O'Biren
Edward S. Ellis
Edwin L. Arnold
Eleanor Atkins
Eleanor Hallowell Abbott
Eliot Gregory
Elizabeth Gaskell
Elizabeth McCracken
Elizabeth Von Arnim
Ellem Key
Emerson Hough
Emilie F. Carlen
Emily Bronte
Emily Dickinson
Enid Bagnold
Enilor Macartney Lane
Erasmus W. Jones
Ernie Howard Pie
Ethel May Dell
Ethel Turner
Ethel Watts Mumford
Eugene Sue
Eugenie Foa
Eugene Wood
Eustace Hale Ball
Evelyn Everett-green
Everard Cotes
F. H. Cheley
F. J. Cross
F. Marion Crawford
Fannie E. Newberry
Federick Austin Ogg
Ferdinand Ossendowski
Fergus Hume
Florence A. Kilpatrick
Fremont B. Deering
Francis Bacon
Francis Darwin
Frances Hodgson Burnett
Frances Parkinson Keyes
Frank Gee Patchin
Frank Harris
Frank Jewett Mather
Frank L. Packard
Frank V. Webster
Frederic Stewart Isham
Frederick Trevor Hill
Frederick Winslow Taylor

Friedrich Kerst
Friedrich Nietzsche
Fyodor Dostoyevsky
G.A. Henty
G.K. Chesterton
Gabrielle E. Jackson
Garrett P. Serviss
Gaston Leroux
George A. Warren
George Ade
Geroge Bernard Shaw
George Cary Eggleston
George Durston
George Ebers
George Eliot
George Gissing
George MacDonald
George Meredith
George Orwell
George Sylvester Viereck
George Tucker
George W. Cable
George Wharton James
Gertrude Atherton
Gordon Casserly
Grace E. King
Grace Gallatin
Grace Greenwood
Grant Allen
Guillermo A. Sherwell
Gulielma Zollinger
Gustav Flaubert
H. A. Cody
H. B. Irving
H.C. Bailey
H. G. Wells
H. H. Munro
H. Irving Hancock
H. R. Naylor
H. Rider Haggard
H. W. C. Davis
Haldeman Julius
Hall Caine
Hamilton Wright Mabie
Hans Christian Andersen
Harold Avery
Harold McGrath
Harriet Beecher Stowe
Harry Castlemon
Harry Coghill
Harry Houidini

Hayden Carruth
Helent Hunt Jackson
Helen Nicolay
Hendrik Conscience
Hendy David Thoreau
Henri Barbusse
Henrik Ibsen
Henry Adams
Henry Ford
Henry Frost
Henry James
Henry Jones Ford
Henry Seton Merriman
Henry W Longfellow
Herbert A. Giles
Herbert Carter
Herbert N. Casson
Herman Hesse
Hildegard G. Frey
Homer
Honore De Balzac
Horace B. Day
Horace Walpole
Horatio Alger Jr.
Howard Pyle
Howard R. Garis
Hugh Lofting
Hugh Walpole
Humphry Ward
Ian Maclaren
Inez Haynes Gillmore
Irving Bacheller
Isabel Cecilia Williams
Isabel Hornibrook
Israel Abrahams
Ivan Turgenev
J.G.Austin
J. Henri Fabre
J. M. Barrie
J. M. Walsh
J. Macdonald Oxley
J. R. Miller
J. S. Fletcher
J. S. Knowles
J. Storer Clouston
J. W. Duffield
Jack London
Jacob Abbott
James Allen
James Andrews
James Baldwin

James Branch Cabell
James DeMille
James Joyce
James Lane Allen
James Lane Allen
James Oliver Curwood
James Oppenheim
James Otis
James R. Driscoll
Jane Abbott
Jane Austen
Jane L. Stewart
Janet Aldridge
Jens Peter Jacobsen
Jerome K. Jerome
Jessie Graham Flower
John Buchan
John Burroughs
John Cournos
John F. Kennedy
John Gay
John Glasworthy
John Habberton
John Joy Bell
John Kendrick Bangs
John Milton
John Philip Sousa
John Taintor Foote
Jonas Lauritz Idemil Lie
Jonathan Swift
Joseph A. Altsheler
Joseph Carey
Joseph Conrad
Joseph E. Badger Jr
Joseph Hergesheimer
Joseph Jacobs
Jules Vernes
Julian Hawthrone
Julie A Lippmann
Justin Huntly McCarthy
Kakuzo Okakura
Karle Wilson Baker
Kate Chopin
Kenneth Grahame
Kenneth McGaffey
Kate Langley Bosher
Kate Langley Bosher
Katherine Cecil Thurston
Katherine Stokes
L. A. Abbot
L. T. Meade

L. Frank Baum
Latta Griswold
Laura Dent Crane
Laura Lee Hope
Laurence Housman
Lawrence Beasley
Leo Tolstoy
Leonid Andreyev
Lewis Carroll
Lewis Sperry Chafer
Lilian Bell
Lloyd Osbourne
Louis Hughes
Louis Joseph Vance
Louis Tracy
Louisa May Alcott
Lucy Fitch Perkins
Lucy Maud Montgomery
Luther Benson
Lydia Miller Middleton
Lyndon Orr
M. Corvus
M. H. Adams
Margaret E. Sangster
Margret Howth
Margaret Vandercook
Margaret W. Hungerford
Margret Penrose
Maria Edgeworth
Maria Thompson Daviess
Mariano Azuela
Marion Polk Angellotti
Mark Overton
Mark Twain
Mary Austin
Mary Catherine Crowley
Mary Cole
Mary Hastings Bradley
Mary Roberts Rinehart
Mary Rowlandson
M. Wollstonecraft Shelley
Maud Lindsay
Max Beerbohm
Myra Kelly
Nathaniel Hawthrone
Nicolo Machiavelli
O. F. Walton
Oscar Wilde

Owen Johnson
P.G. Wodehouse
Paul and Mabel Thorne
Paul G. Tomlinson
Paul Severing
Percy Brebner
Percy Keese Fitzhugh
Peter B. Kyne
Plato
Quincy Allen
R. Derby Holmes
R. L. Stevenson
R. S. Ball
Rabindranath Tagore
Rahul Alvares
Ralph Bonehill
Ralph Henry Barbour
Ralph Victor
Ralph Waldo Emmerson
Rene Descartes
Ray Cummings
Rex Beach
Rex E. Beach
Richard Harding Davis
Richard Jefferies
Richard Le Gallienne
Robert Barr
Robert Frost
Robert Gordon Anderson
Robert L. Drake
Robert Lansing
Robert Lynd
Robert Michael Ballantyne
Robert W. Chambers
Rosa Nouchette Carey
Rudyard Kipling
Saint Augustine
Samuel B. Allison
Samuel Hopkins Adams
Sarah Bernhardt
Sarah C. Hallowell
Selma Lagerlof
Sherwood Anderson
Sigmund Freud
Standish O'Grady
Stanley Weyman
Stella Benson
Stella M. Francis

Stephen Crane
Stewart Edward White
Stijn Streuvels
Swami Abhedananda
Swami Parmananda
T. S. Ackland
T. S. Arthur
The Princess Der Ling
Thomas A. Janvier
Thomas A Kempis
Thomas Anderton
Thomas Bailey Aldrich
Thomas Bulfinch
Thomas De Quincey
Thomas Dixon
Thomas H. Huxley
Thomas Hardy
Thomas More
Thornton W. Burgess
U. S. Grant
Upton Sinclair
Valentine Williams
Various Authors
Vaughan Kester
Victor Appleton
Victor G. Durham
Victoria Cross
Virginia Woolf
Wadsworth Camp
Walter Camp
Walter Scott
Washington Irving
Wilbur Lawton
Wilkie Collins
Willa Cather
Willard F. Baker
William Dean Howells
William le Queux
W. Makepeace Thackeray
William W. Walter
William Shakespeare
Winston Churchill
Yei Theodora Ozaki
Yogi Ramacharaka
Young E. Allison
Zane Grey